# NEVER AGAIN A WORLD WITHOUT US

## VOICES OF MAYAN WOMEN
## IN CHIAPAS, MEXICO

### BY TERESA ORTIZ

**EPICA**

*Never Again a World Without Us*
© 2001 by EPICA
The Ecumenical Program on Central America and the Caribbean (EPICA)
1470 Irving St. NW, Washington, DC 20010
(202) 332-0292; fax (202)332-1184
e-mail: epica@igc.org
web page: www.epica.org

An EPICA book
All rights reserved.

Cover photo: A community mural in Chiapas captured on film by Teresa Ortiz
Book and cover design: Ann Butwell
Maps: Ruth Butwell, Kathy Ogle & Ann Butwell
Proofreading: Siobhán Dugan & Erin Yost

## Library of Congress Cataloging-in-Publication Data

Ortiz, Teresa, 1948-
   Never again a world without us: voices of Mayan women in Chiapas,
   Mexico / by Teresa Ortiz.
      p. cm.
   ISBN 0-918346-26-6 (pbk.)
      1. Maya women--Mexico--Chiapas--Social conditions. 2. Chiapas (Mexico)--
History--Peasant uprising, 1994- 3. Maya Indians--Mexico--Chiapas--
Government relations. 4. Chiapas (Mexico)--Social conditions. I. Ecumenical
Program on Central America and the Caribbean. II. Title.

F1435.3.W55 078 2001
972'.750835--dc21                                                      00-067714

*A Gabriel Dominic,*
*A Aaron Marley,*
*A Carmen Maya,*
*con todo mi amor, por siempre.*

*A todos los y todas las niñ@s y jóvenes de Chiapas,*
*semillas y flores del futuro.*

To Gabriel Dominic,
To Aaron Marley,
To Carmen Maya,
with all my love, forever.

To all the children and youth of Chiapas,
seeds and buds of the future.

✴

# ACKNOWLEDGMENTS

KOLABAL!

*Kolabal* means thank you in the Mayan languages of Tzotzil and Tzeltal. Because this project has been a collective effort of many people who assisted me every step of the way, I want to say *kolabal*. I was not the only author of this book. Mostly, it is a gift from the Mayan people of Chiapas whose voices were recorded, translated and turned here into written words. To all the people who trusted me enough to tell your story of labor and struggle, I want to say *kolabal*. This book—my tiny contribution of solidarity in the struggle for peace in Chiapas—is for all of you.

This book started as an idea in 1995, when I moved with my family to Chiapas from Guatemala. It was originally the idea of my husband, Tomás Johnson, who thought it was important to tell the story of Chiapas in the voices of the Mayan people, who are the real participants in the struggle. Tomás helped me to write the general outline for the book, to write a funding proposal for the research and to contact community authorities to get their permission for the interviews. He also supported my efforts during the years of research and writing. *Kolabal*, Tomás. To my children, *muchísimas gracias* for your patience and for your love.

I want to say *gracias* to my dear friend Mercedes Olivera, a Mexican anthropologist and feminist, who sat with me in the first stages of the book and patiently helped me map out a strategy of where to start and where to go from there, and for helping with the contacts for interviews. *Gracias* also go to my Mexican Chiapan friends: Gerardo González who sent me to Morelia with a letter from the non-governmental organization CONPAZ in hand; to Alejandra Alvarez and Roger Maldonado who provided background information on Morelia and to Abraham who accompanied me in my first trip there; to Rosario who went with me to Ejido Emiliano Zapata; to Carlota Duarte from the Archivo Fotográfico Indigena, to the women of CIAM, to the women of FOMMA and Jolom Mayatik, to the people of SIPAZ, and to Las Abejas de Chenalho'. *Kolabal* to the community people for your patience and assistance in oral translations from Chol, Tzotzil and Tzeltal, and especially to Alonso of *Las Abejas*, for his many hours at the computer with transcriptions and translations from Tzeltal and Tzotzil into Spanish. To the many Mexicans and internationalists in Chiapas, visitors, observers, accompaniers, and workers that I met in my travels and work: thanks for your encouragement and for the great times. I also want to express my admiration for your commitment, solidarity, courage and dedication. And if I don't mention you all, it is because it still is difficult and dangerous to be on the side of peace in Chiapas and I could get you in trouble. However, I want to at least mention just one valiant woman, Maria Darlington. Thanks for our conversations, wonderful times, midnight excursions, and for your great work.

I want especially to thank my very good friend Nancy Black, anthropologist and specialist in Mayan women, who helped me organize the book, did the initial editing and who guided me to look for publishing possibilities. Several friends, Chiapas experts, Latin-Americanists and writers read the manuscript at different stages, providing critical comments and assistance. I want to thank Jan Gasco and Jerry Moore, Jan and Diane Rus, and Christine Ebert, as well as Carla Hagen, Shelley Sherman and Monika Firl for your comments and support. Y *muchísimas gracias y un abrazo fuerte* to Oscar Hernández for your help with the final stages of the book.

I want to give my heartfelt thanks to Children's Haven for the economic support in 1997 to do extensive research that helped me travel throughout Chiapas and interview people in their communities and towns. Thank you Harold, Louise and Christine for believing in the importance of this research and this book. I want to thank the board, past and present staff and volunteers of my organization, Cloudforest Initiatives, for your continued support, help and encouragement throughout my work. Since this is just another contribution to my work in Chiapas, this is your book.

Finally, I want to give special thanks to the Ecumenical Program on Central America and the Caribbean (EPICA), for believing in this book from the beginning, supporting my work, and wanting to publish the testimonies of the Mayan people of Chiapas. Thank you to Phil Wheaton, Lynn Yellott and Julia Dietz for their comments on the draft copy and *muchas gracias* Anita Butwell, Scott Wright and Kathy Ogle. *Gracias* especially to Kathy, my editor, for the long hours working on the final revisions of this book.

# CONTENTS

✳

## FOREWORD

Five hundred years ago, present day Mexico belonged to indigenous peoples. Then with the Spanish conquest came the brutal colonial system of slavery and exploitation. Neither independence from Spain nor the Mexican revolution managed to reverse the lethal grip of racism and domination left by the conquest. Power changed hands for centuries without ever including the indigenous poor in decision-making or control over the resources that surrounded them. Indigenous people resisted as best they could, laboring on plantations, migrating to new frontiers for land and holding fast to their languages and cultural traditions

Finally, at the dawn of the 21st century, a cry arose in the southern state of Chiapas, a cry that might be paraphrased in the following words: "You cannot continue to 'modernize' the country without consulting us. You cannot take away our land and extract precious minerals from beneath our feet, pretending that we don't exist. You cannot make decisions to end our way of life—our communal existence, our traditions, our rural economies—by saying that it is inevitable. You cannot relegate us to museums and whitewashed history books. We will not go."

It took an armed uprising of the Zapatista National Liberation Army (EZLN) to punctuate these kinds of simple statements of dignified resistance and shake Mexican society to the core. When this barefoot indigenous army rose up on January 1, 1994 —the same day that the North American Free Trade Agreement (NAFTA) took effect—the Mexican government tried to crush the rebellion quickly and keep it out of the news. Why? War would be bad for business. It would discourage the foreign investment they were trying to attract. Besides, the Zapatistas' ideas were diametrically opposed to the neoliberal economic model to which the Mexican government was already deeply committed. The success of a neoliberal model depended on *less* citizen participation, not more. It relied on *less* social spending, not more. It planned to *end* the rural way of life, not support it. And, it planned to give control of natural resources over to transnational corporations, not to indigenous communities.

But the Mexican government was not successful in crushing the Zapatistas or in keeping their movement out of the news. Over the last six years, national and international pressure for negotiations with the Zapatistas has increased, and human rights groups have focused their attention on the region, making it difficult for the Mexican Army to overtly attack the Zapatistas' civilian base of support. Rather than negotiate in good faith with the Zapatistas, however, the Mexican government has only given lip-service to the idea. The San Andrés accords on Indigenous Rights and Culture, signed in February 1996, remain only words on paper as the government has refused to sign them into law.

Meanwhile, with the help of the United States, the Mexican government has implemented a strategy of low-intensity warfare in Chiapas to wear down Zapatista supporters and create division in their ranks. To date, tens of thousands of indigenous people have been displaced from their lands in a covert war carried out by paramilitary groups linked to the military, to landowners and to local power structures of the official Institutional Revolutionary Party (PRI). It is a dirty war that its perpetrators try to keep out of the news. Yet it threatens to accelerate the destruction of the indigenous cultural fabric, economic base and way of life.

The "low-intensity war" in Chiapas today is a war against civilians. This means that men, women and children are directly affected. Women are affected in a particular way as those who raise and protect their children and do most of the household chores. In a recent trip to Chiapas, EPICA staff met with members of Center for Research and Action on Women (CIAM). They told us that the presence of the Mexican Army in Chiapas has increased in recent months and changed from being temporary encampments to permanent outposts near many indigenous communities, especially those suspected of being sympathetic to the Zapatistas. Because of violent army incursions in the past, and because of army ties to local paramilitary groups, the nearby presence of soldiers strikes fear into hearts of the community people, especially women.

Soldiers harass women verbally and try to get information from children. They constrain free movement in and out of the community through arbitrary questioning. Rumors of rape cause stress and tension. Army giveaway programs aimed at winning hearts and minds also tend to be directed at women and children. At the same time, soldiers use the community's water and cut its wood, thereby increasing women's work loads. Prostitution near the army posts heightens the sense of insecurity for indigenous women. In addition, religious practices and cultural traditions have been interrupted by the violent uprooting of communities and harassment experienced during religious rituals and feast days.[1] As this book goes to press, 60,000 Mexican soldiers are still in Chiapas, and paramilitary groups continue to operate with impunity.

### The Intent of this Book

The resistance of indigenous people who clamor for change in Mexico is not based on any military strength they might have to win a war against the Mexican government. It is based on their cultural identity and organization, and their capacity to focus world attention on their plight. Within this context, indigenous women and men have entrusted Teresa Ortiz with their stories for this book. Their desire is for the world to know more about what they are going through and what their hopes are for the future. Their hope is encapsulated in the title of the book, *Never Again A World Without Us*—the desire to fully participate in the decisions that affect their lives.

The voices projected here are not exclusively those of women, but the emphasis on women is strong because of the fact that women's

---

[1] See "Women and Low Intensity Warfare" in the Appendices.

opinions and priorities have so often been left out of previous revolutionary movements and from literature in general. *Never Again A World Without Us* is the cry of indigenous people, and it is particularly the cry of indigenous women who are only just beginning to win spaces for equal participation in their own communities. In Mexico, as in the rest of Latin America, indigenous women are the most marginalized and exploited. They are at the very bottom of most social indicators that measure health, longevity, education, nutrition and literacy. This book seeks to empower these indigenous women by recording and projecting their voices, their hopes and their dreams. It is a task that is nobly accomplished through the author's skill and her ability to win the confidence of those she has interviewed.

Each chapter of *Never Again A World Without Us* contains the testimony of one or more people with whom the author has spent hours of time. They are Mayan indigenous people—primarily women— who tell us about their communities and their lives. Not surprisingly, the array of voices carries complex and intertwining messages. Some of those interviewed are direct supporters of the Zapatista movement, and all of them have been affected by it in some way. Some speak as poor people struggling for land and economic justice. Some speak as women who are organizing for the right to develop themselves and participate equally with men. Some speak as indigenous Mayans who want to preserve their traditional decision-making systems. Still others speak as outraged victims of violence. In each chapter, the author provides us with history and context for the interviews and then turns the floor over to the women.

### How the Book is Organized

Through the course of this book, we accompany Teresa Ortiz on her journey from the Lacandón rainforest, to the highlands, to the canyon region of *Las Cañadas,* and to the remote grasslands area of northern Chiapas. In each chapter, the author provides the background information necessary for understanding the context of the interviews. She then lets us know some of her own thoughts and perspectives as she introduces us to the people whose voices we are about to hear. As we finish each chapter, we feel as though we have gotten to know the women and men who have spoken to us, and we wonder what their future will be.

In Chapter One, María, a Tzotzil homesteader in the Lacandón rainforest, tells us her story. Here the history of the government plan to colonize the jungle is laid out in all of its complexities and contradictions. This is the jungle where the Zapatista Army was born and to which it retreats. When we put down this book to read in today's newspaper of the Mexican army surrounding the jungle to "build roads" or "plant trees," we will think of María and how this militarization is affecting her and her community.

In Chapter Two we move to the highland city of San Cristóbal de las Casas, a tourist haven in the midst of the war. Quickly, however, we are led into a behind-the-scenes look at the city's multilayered class structure, evolved from racist colonial times. We meet three young indigenous women—Xunka', Isabel and Lorenza—who are learning about their rights through their work with various organizations related to the arts. As the three struggle to develop themselves, they hold on to their commitment to be resources for their communities.

In the various sections of Chapter Three, we travel with the author into the heart of Zapatista territory in the highlands, *Las Cañadas* and the rainforest. We hear from community representatives who tell us about their lives, how they are trying to organize into autonomous indigenous communities, and how they have been attacked and harassed by the Mexican Army. They speak of the Zapatista "Laws of Women" and how these laws are changing women's lives.

In Chapter Six we sit with the author outside of the government building in the state capital of Tuxtla Gutiérrez. With us are hundreds of Chol Indians from northern Chiapas who are protesting the paramilitary war in their communities. They have been pushed off their lands, and many of their loved ones have been killed or unjustly imprisoned. As we hear about local conflicts, the attacks on church catechists and independent political groups, we get a sense of the abusive local power structures related to the PRI party. We also get an idea of how government structures are complicit in promoting paramilitary groups such as *Paz y Justicia* in order to divide and wear down any opposition.

In Chapter Seven, Alonso, a Tzotzil refugee in San Cristóbal, tells us about the indigenous pacifist organization, *Las Abejas*—The Bees. He speaks with a tone of urgency since paramilitary groups have just attacked his community and run them off their lands. He does not know if his wife is dead or alive. Meanwhile, threats and violent actions against civilian Zapatista and *Abejas* communities are growing in the highlands. Everyday the *Abejas* go to the local authorities to denounce the violence, but nobody lifts a finger to stop it. We listen with growing horror to Alonso's final interview given just one day before the massacre at Acteal, and we begin to realize that no one will intervene to stop it. Another *Abejas* catechist named José describes the heart-rending scene the morning after. The chapter ends as we attend the funeral with the author, and wonder what it will take to stop this madness.

### A Final Word

This book does not pretend to cover the entire history of Mexico or even that of Chiapas. Rather than a complete resource on Chiapas, it should be seen as an introduction—a way of arousing interest in the region through the personal and very human stories of courageous indigenous women and men. Most chapters include some updates on what has happened in each community since the interviews were held. In addition, the appendix provides a chronology of events in Chiapas, some recent analysis and a list of organizations to contact for more information.

It is our hope that the voices of the women and men interviewed in this book will inspire the reader to learn more about the struggle taking place in Chiapas. Behind the poverty, the uprising, the government response, the pain and the displacement of indigenous people evident in these chapters, lie the root causes of the conflict. To delve into those causes means to learn more about NAFTA and about the global economic system.

What role do large corporations and the United States government play in determining the rules of free trade? What can communities do to defend their economic and cultural interests and ensure a place for themselves in decision-making about their own futures? How can civil society be strengthened to challenge the domination of corporate interests? How can communities themselves become more democratic, allowing a diversity of voices and the participation of both women and men? And how might we, as readers, take steps to be in solidarity with the indigenous people of Chiapas like those interviewed here? Our hope is that this book may be a catalyst for asking these questions and moving to action.

# CHIAPAS, MEXICO

MEXICO

Chiapas

**Chiapas is the 8th largest state in Mexico and the state with the highest levels of poverty. Almost one million indigenous people are among the state's 3.5 million population.**

Sources: Secretary of the Treasury of Chiapas and the National Population Commission (CONAPO).

# Indigenous Language Groups of Chiapas

Veracruz

Tabasco

GUATEMALA

Language Groups
1. Tzotzil
2. Tojolobal
3. Chol
4. Tzeltal
5. Zoque
6. Mame, Moche & Kachiquel

# GEOGRAPHICAL REGIONS OF CHIAPAS

Regions
1. The Lacandón Rainforest/*La Selva*
(area inside the dotted line is the Monte Azules Bioreserve)
2. The Highlands/*Los Altos*
3. The Canyon Area/*Las Cañadas*
4. Northern Area/*El Norte*

✳

# ONE

# Homesteading in the Lacandón Rainforest

# Introduction:
# The Road to the Rainforest

Doña María repeated the first phrase of her story several times: "Yes, yes, 1968 was the year. It was in August 1968 that we walked to the jungle. It was in 1968 that we built this community called Emiliano Zapata here in the Lacandón rainforest."

She was sitting in front of me at her kitchen table, a beautiful, thin, 40-year-old woman wearing a blue satin dress. She had just come back from the river, where she bathed and washed her clothes. After a day of working in the cornfield under the radiant sun and humid heat of the tropics, she had decided to stop at the river on her way home so she could clean up and change into her best dress. She knew I was coming to see her this afternoon.

The evening breeze was finally cooling off what had been an unbearably hot day. We could hear a loud chattering as a flock of parrots flew overhead on its evening trip home. Nearby, children ran and played, climbing trees or rolling in the mud. Then they washed each other off by throwing cool buckets of water at each other. A sweet smell of tropical fruits and flowers covered the air. A simple house—just one room and a kitchen, built of wood with a dirt floor— María's home was set in a tropical paradise and surrounded by all kinds of fruit trees: mangos, avocados, limes, tangerines and *chicozapotes.*[1]

María's mother, an old woman in her eighties with long white braids and the traditional dress of her hometown in the highlands, sat in her favorite wooden chair shelling corn. María's adult daughter was lying in a hammock, swinging for a few precious, lazy moments before going back to her daily household chores. Her job was to care for a half dozen children, to clean, wash, sweep, cook, to grind the corn and the coffee beans, to carry wood from the forest and to carry water from the river. In a few minutes she would have to start dinner for her family and her guests.

---

[1]*Chicozapotes*—the fruit of the gum tree.

"Yes, yes," Doña María repeated because I kept asking her the same question. "That was the year, yes, 1968." I kept thinking that it was an incredible coincidence that 1968 was the year it all started for this family, for this town. Many of the communities this side of the Lacandón forest had sprung up in that year. But 1968 had been a defining year for my own life as well, and one I'd always considered a watershed year for Mexican history. For me, and for many Mexicans of my generation, 1968 was the year when everything in Mexico changed forever.

As I listened to María describe how they had literally walked from the northern Chiapas highlands to the rainforest, how they'd built this paradise from nothing, and how they'd organized to defend their rights, I thought of what had happened that same year in the country's capital. I remembered our marches in Mexico City, the meetings and assemblies to organize students and teachers, the demands that political prisoners be freed and that restitution be paid to the families of students who had been killed or injured. I also remembered the excitement of feeling that we were part of Mexican history, and that our actions might bring about democracy and social change. Then finally, there was the massacre of hundreds of student protesters on October 2 in Tlatelolco plaza.[2]

### The Generation of 1968

Most analysts would agree that indeed, 1968 was a watershed year in modern Mexican history. For many urban Mexicans, the Popular Student Movement of 1968 and the subsequent repression marked the end of an era. Although the legitimacy of the Mexican one-party state had been questioned for decades by unions, peasant farmer groups and the traditional left, it was not until the late 1960s that protests became more widespread, igniting national movements that spread throughout Mexico. The government responded with repression, which culminated in the Tlatelolco massacre and left a volatile wake of anger and disillusionment.

---

[2]For an excellent account of the events of October 1968 in Tlatelolco, Mexico, see Elena Poniatowska, *Massacre in Mexico* (St. Louis: University of Missouri Press, 1992).

The so-called "Generation of 1968"—students, activists, intellectuals, members of traditional Marxist organizations and progressive workers' unions, as well as thousands of urban middle and working class youth—left universities and discussion groups to join the urban and rural poor in their neighborhoods and communities. They helped to organize rural subsistence farmers (*campesinos*) and urban dwellers to defend their civil rights and demand democratic change. Many members of this generation had seen years of political organizing fail to bring social change. They believed that transformations in Mexico could only come about with armed revolutionary struggle. An underground urban and rural guerrilla movement grew and began to flourish throughout Mexico in the 1970s. By the mid-1980s, however, it was almost completely crushed by the brutal repression of the Mexican security forces.[3]

The struggle of the 1970s and 1980s, however, would define the future. One of the guerrilla groups—the National Liberation Forces (FLN)—became the core group that went to the Chiapas Lacandón rainforest in 1983 to organize what later became the Zapatista National Liberation Army, or EZLN. Another group of the "Generation of 1968," believing that change could only come from within the system, joined government forces to promote the implementation of social policies that would benefit *campesinos* and workers.[4]

In 1970, Luís Echeverría became President of Mexico. He had been the Minister of the Interior at the time of the Tlatelolco massacre, and was accused of direct complicity in the massacre as well as in other atrocities committed by that administration. After a second massacre of students occurred during Echeverría's administration in 1971, the resulting outrage forced Echeverría to try to clean up his image. Consequently, federal government policies in the 1970s were characterized by attempts to pacify the discontent coming from the left—that is from workers, *campesinos*, urban dwellers, students and activists. While some of the measures taken caused the private sector

---

[3] Tom Barry, *Zapata's Revenge: Free Trade and the Farm Crisis in Mexico* (Boston: South End Press, 1995).
[4] Ibid.

to label Echeverría a populist, the policies did little to improve the actual economic situation of the majority of Mexicans.

In the countryside, Echeverría turned government attention to the agrarian sector, promoting *campesino* organizations and rural development programs, implementing new agrarian policies and encouraging the creation of new *ejido* associations.[5] These policies did not change the political and economic structure in the rural areas because they did not touch the economic interests of the powerful rural elite—the landowners, cattle ranchers and logging companies. In fact, these policies were not ever directed at solving the root causes of injustice. Their true objective was to co-opt *campesino* groups and to bring them into the structure of the Institutional Revolutionary Party (PRI).[6] Together with the activism that swept through the countryside in those years, however, these agrarian policies also facilitated the growth of new *campesino* movements.[7] Many of the communities in the rainforest were created, grew and flourished in the 1970s.

### People in Motion

It would be wrong, however, to say that it was the "outside forces" of the student movement or government policies that created

---

[5]*ejido* associations—The Agrarian Laws in Article 27 of the 1917 Mexican Constitution gave landless peasant farmers the right to request land communally from the government. This land, called an *ejido*, was communally owned and could be inherited but not sold. *Ejido* communities became villages with their own authorities, including a representative of the government, who dealt with agrarian issues.

[6]The Institutional Revolutionary Party (PRI) has dominated Mexico's political life since its founding in 1929. Originally called the National Revolutionary Party, the party was renamed the Mexican Revolutionary Party in 1938 and took its current name in 1946. Various presidents consolidated PRI power in different ways. Echeverría's policies of creating unions and agrarian groups caused many communities throughout Mexico to become PRI supporters. From the party's founding in 1929 until the year 2000, every president of Mexico was a member of the PRI. In 2000 this changed with the election of Vicente Fox of the PAN party.

[7]Yvon Le Bot, *Subcomandante Marcos: El Sueño Zapatista* (Barcelona: Plaza & Janés, 1997) p. 35.

*campesino* activism and organizing in the Lacandón rainforest. The Mayan indigenous people of Chiapas have a long history of survival and resistance, of organizing and adapting. Our history books tell us that the ancestors of the Lacandón homesteaders created one of the great civilizations of the ancient world in this rain forest. The remains of this civilization can still be admired in the lost cities of the jungle, such as Bonampak and Palenque on the Mexican side of the Lacandón area, and in Tikal just across the border in Guatemala.

At the time of the Spanish conquest, Mayan Indians held the best coastal lowlands. They were almost immediately pushed into the highlands by the Spanish colonizers and were forced to cultivate their traditional crops of corn, beans and squash on the sides of mountains, on land not suited for agriculture. In order to survive, the highland Mayans of Chiapas have always had to migrate seasonally to work for cash on plantations in the coastal plains or in northern Chiapas.

During the first half of the 20th century, however, with conditions in the highlands worsening, thousands of Mayan Tzotziles and Tzeltales actually moved to northern Chiapas.[8] They were recruited to work on plantations or they went in search of land to work as sharecroppers. Maria's parents and grandparents were part of this migration, moving from the highlands to work on plantations in Simojovel, Sabanilla and Huitiupan.

In the 1940s and 1950s, and particularly during the administration of President Lázaro Cárdenas in the 1940s, new *ejidos* were created throughout Mexico. However, the *ejido* system failed to provide land to thousands of landless *campesinos*, especially in places like Chiapas, where large tracts of private land were not touched. Cattle ranching replaced plantation agriculture on many of these large holdings, diminishing the need for a massive work force. Thus, many farm workers were pushed off of the plantations to look for work or

---

[8]There are seven indigenous groups in Chiapas, Mexico, six of which are Mayan. Each indigenous group has its own language, customs and traditions. The Tzotzil people of the highlands and the Tzeltal, who live in the highlands and *Las Cañadas*, are two of the six Mayan groups in Chiapas.

land to rent elsewhere.

As María's story will show us, one of the government solutions to the pressure for land was to open up the rainforest for colonization. And just as it happened in the Ixcán and Petén forests of Guatemala, in the Amazon jungle of Brazil and in other regions of the Americas, the rainforest solution created more problems than it solved. María's family's history of determination, pioneering, and struggle is fascinating precisely because it is not a unique story in the history of the Lacandón jungle.

### *Landless Peasants Encouraged to Clear the Jungle*

When the government decided to open up rainforest land to landless *campesinos*, it provided groups of *campesinos* with *ejido*—or communally owned—land tracts. For the *campesinos*, even this first step was often a never-ending game of paperwork. In Chiapas, for instance, they had to make continuous trips to the state capital, Tuxtla Gutiérrez, to obtain *ejido* titles in a process that consumed inordinate amounts of their time, resources and energy. Even today, there are thousands of unresolved cases of land ownership that have been sitting in state and federal agrarian offices for years. Because of corruption and mismanagement on the part of government officials, there are many cases where several "owners" claim the same land with either *ejido* documents or personal titles.

Once they had the promise of—if not the documents for—the land, the *campesino* settlers had to find a way to get to the land, set up provisional housing, clear the forest and then till the land for cultivation. Once the land was cleared, however, its commercial value increased, and it was common for private parties who wanted the land for cattle ranching or commercial farming to try to purchase it from the settlers, legally or illegally. Cattle ranching and commercial farming depleted the soil even further, and the homesteaders who sold their plots often moved deeper into the rainforest, clearing more land.

A series of problems emerged from this process. The cattle ranchers and plantation owners who claimed the same land as the *campesinos* felt they needed to protect the land against takeovers.

They trained private guards—called "white guards" in Chiapas—to protect their properties and harass *campesinos*. The *ejido* farmers were at a disadvantage with respect to the cattle ranchers and commercial farmers, but they organized into unions and associations to demand that the government speed up the transfer of their land titles. They pushed for more land for their offspring and for new arrivals, and they requested government subsidies, agricultural technical assistance and community development aid. The *campesinos* also retaliated against the attacks of the white guards and against the greed of ranchers and rich farmers who continued to buy up and take over the land that they had cleared.

Thus, the same problems that existed in the agricultural areas where the *campesinos* came from were imported to the new frontier. The demand for land persisted and increased, and the conflicts between *campesinos* and ranchers often escalated into violent confrontations.

### The Environment vs. the Settlers?

As the new agrarian communities sprouted in the jungle, large-scale commercial logging of precious tropical timber was also happening. Logging had been going on in the Lacandón rainforest for almost a century, but it wasn't until the 1970s that the government gave logging companies permission to extract great quantities of valuable lumber. Widespread illegal logging also started in those years, as logging companies paid poor *ejido* dwellers badly needed cash to extract the precious lumber from their land. In those years the Lacandón jungle was deforested rapidly, valuable timber resources disappeared, and the rainforest frontier was pushed closer to the Guatemalan border. Today the Petén rainforest in Guatemala is relatively lush compared to the massively deforested Lacandón jungle on the Mexican side of the border.

*Campesinos* are often blamed for the disappearance of the rainforest. Environmentalists talk about the damage caused by "slash and burn" agriculture, as well as damage caused by constant immigration into the virgin forest. However, even greater deforestation of the rainforest has been caused by cattle raising, large-scale commercial farming, and legal and illegal logging. After having encouraged immigration into the jungle, the government of Mexico began to reverse its policy, claiming concern for the preservation of the rainforest and for the survival of a small group of indigenous Mayans who had always lived in the forest—the Lacandón Indians. This apparent concern for the environment and for indigenous people hid underlying political and economic interests—the desire to control forestry and bio-diversity resources, hydroelectric power, and oil reserves in the rainforest.

Two governmental actions changed the course of history for the homesteaders of the Lacandón rainforest. In 1972, President Echeverría decreed that a territory of 600,000 hectares[9] be given to 66 Lacandón Mayan families. Meanwhile, the hundreds of thousands of Tzeltal, Tzotzil, Chol, Tojolabal, Zoque and *mestizo campesinos,* who had recently homesteaded the area and held legal titles to their land, were to be pushed out. In 1977, the Montes Azules Bioreserve was established on Lacandón Indian land and in some of the new *campesino* colonies.

The establishment of this bioreserve also threatened to push the new settlers from their rainforest homes. In her story, Doña María says that most of the *ejidos* were not inside the reserve. Still the homesteaders feared eviction by the government and security forces. Out of fear of eviction, many *campesinos* left the area to form communities elsewhere. The majority of settlers, however, stayed in the rainforest to defend their new land and their dream.[10]

### The Promised Land

The settlers came into the forest looking not only for land, but also for a new life. They brought with them two valuable tools for

---

[9]hectare—a measurement of land equal to 10,000 square meters or 2.471 acres. (600,000 hectares equals approximately one and a half million acres.)

[10]Yvon Le Bot, *Subcomandante Marcos: El Sueño Zapatista*, pp. 54-55. In his analysis, based on his interview with Subcomandante Marcos, Le Bot uses the word, "dream" to describe the process of organizing and struggle in the rainforest, as well as the Zapatista struggle in subsequent years.

survival: their ancient Indian culture and their deep Christian faith. The indigenous people of Chiapas, fleeing from lives of misery and oppression on plantations and marginal lands, considered themselves the chosen and persecuted People of God. The Lacandón rainforest became for them "the Promised Land" where they could achieve their spiritual, political, economic and ethnic liberation. It was a Garden of Eden where they were to build the kingdom of heaven on earth— a place of freedom from their oppressors, of peace and harmony, of brotherhood and prosperity. Mayans and other indigenous people from all over Chiapas, as well as many landless indigenous *campesinos* from Oaxaca, Veracruz, Tabasco and Michoacán came to the Lacandón rainforest. This was a Tower of Babel where speakers of many languages were supposed to live like brothers and sisters.

The Catholic Diocese of San Cristóbal, headed by Bishop Samuel Ruíz, was the institution that provided the most support for the indigenous people of Chiapas in their struggle for land and for justice. Within the growing tradition of liberation theology, the Catholic Church of Bishop Ruíz combined the spirituality and traditions of the Mayan people with a "preferential option for the poor."[11] These became key elements in the rapid transformations that occurred throughout indigenous communities. The impact of the Church was felt especially in the new settlements of the rainforest and *Las Cañadas*[12] where hundreds of indigenous Catholic lay workers called

---

[11]Liberation theology promotes the idea that God desires both spiritual and material liberation for the poor. This theology grew and flourished throughout Latin America in the 1960s, 1970s and 1980s as priests, religious and layworkers of the Catholic Church began to work more closely with poor communities. Their experiences influenced the documents that came out of bishops' conferences in Medellín, Colombia (1968) and Puebla, México (1974), in which the Church was encouraged to abandon its traditional alliances with powerful groups in favor of a "preferential option for the poor."

[12]*Las Cañadas* is one of the geographical areas of Chiapas. It is a system of deep canyons and ravines that connects the highlands area with the Lacandón rainforest.

catechists[13] went from community to community promoting a new kind of Bible study. In this new experience, Christians would gather in community meetings and reflect on the oppression they'd experienced, dream about a new world on this earth and talk about how to struggle for a better life. The work of the catechists was not merely to save souls, but rather to raise awareness about the political and economic slavery in which the people had lived for centuries.

A rapid process of transformation occurred in the rainforest, in *Las Cañadas* and in the highlands. As the indigenous people worked for their liberation, the Catholic Church was engaging in its own process of transformation. Bible study meetings became village assemblies of the Mayan tradition, in which decisions are made only when everyone present agrees. Remarking on these meetings, Bishop Ruíz said, "Most of us don't have the capacity to understand each other if we all talk at the same time, and yet this is exactly what happens in these assemblies. Everybody talks, they all understand one another, and they reach consensus quickly and with a minimum of conflict. I don't how they do it."[14]

### Political Organizing

One of the biggest organizations formed in the rainforest was the *K'ip Tik Talekumtasel*—Tzeltal for "Our Organization's Strength is for our Liberation." The *K'ip Tik* was a grassroots indigenous movement that grew out of the Indigenous Congress, a state-wide meeting of Indian peoples organized by Bishop Ruíz and the San Cristóbal Diocese in 1974. It was also one of the Rural Collective Union Associations, or credit unions, organized in the 1970s for *ejido* farmers to negotiate collectively with government agrarian and credit institutions. The *K'ip Tik* organization spread throughout the jungle and

---

[13]The Catholic Church has long employed catechists, who are lay leaders charged with teaching Catholic doctrine and preparing people for sacraments such as baptism and first communion. Since the late 1960s, catechists have also been group discussion facilitators for Bible study and community action groups. They have been important in the integration and organization of many isolated indigenous communities in Chiapas.

[14]Bishop Samuel Ruíz, interview with a US Protestant church group, January 1997.

*Las Cañadas*, playing a vital role in organizing, uniting and mobilizing the hundreds of newly formed indigenous communities and *ejidos*. Eventually it became the Rural Association of Collective Interest (ARIC-Union of Unions). By the mid-1980s, the membership of ARIC included around 6,000 families from 130 communities.[15]

The struggle of rainforest homesteaders in the first years was to find, acquire, retain and defend their communal lands from private owners and government interference. In the latter part of the 1970s and early 1980s, objectives extended to obtaining agricultural credits, forming production projects such as coffee cooperatives, and marketing their products. These were the golden years of growth and unity in the jungle communities, when the *K'ip Tik Talekumtasel* flourished as a grassroots, Mayan and Catholic organization.

The Mayan settlers were aided, not only by the Catholic Church,but also by leftist organizers who came into the rainforest in the 1970s. These post-1968 leftists helped the communities to organize into *ejido* unions to support each other and to make demands of the government.[16]

In the late 1970s and early 1980s, a crisis arose in the *K'ip Tik Talekumtasel* when some organizers from a Maoist group called the Popular Front-Proletarian Group tried to take control of the organization. These men were accused of being government agents and were eventually expelled from the rainforest. The accusations were apparently well-founded as some of these same Maoists worked openly for the government in later administrations.[17]

In November 1983, a few months after this crisis in the *K'ip Tik,* another small group of post-1968 leftists came into the Lacandón

---

[15] Tom Barry, p. 161.

[16] Yvon Le Bot, p. 54-58.

[17] In the 1990s, during the Salinas de Gortari administration, several members of this organization were high-level government employees. In 1998, during the Ernesto Zedillo administration, Adolfo Orive—the mastermind of the Proletarian Line—became the main adviser to the Minister of the Interior. Many analysts believe that the counterinsurgency policies of the war in Chiapas have been drafted by Orive, based on his previous knowledge of Chiapas, on his experience with the communities, and on inside information from indigenous organizations.

rainforest. They had been members of the National Liberation Forces (FLN), an urban guerrilla organization made up of middle class students, intellectuals and activists. Through a ten-year process of organizing with the communities of the jungle, *Las Cañadas* and the highlands, this small group grew into the Zapatista Army of National Liberation (EZLN). In the 1980s, the Zapatista movement grew to become more important and extensive than the *K'ip Tik* had been in the 1970s. In 1994, the ARIC again split into two factions, those who agreed with Zapatista demands and those who did not.

The Lacandón rainforest today is populated by thousands of *campesinos* from all over the state of Chiapas and from many other Mexican states. They are indigenous people—Tzeltal and Tzotzil from the highlands, Chol from northern Chiapas, Tojolabal from the border lowlands, Zoque and *mestizos*[18] from the Pacific lowlands, as well as other Indians and *mestizos* from other Mexican states. All of them coexist with a couple hundred Lacandón Mayans, the earliest inhabitants of the rainforest. By the 1990s, approximately two hundred thousand Indians and *mestizos* were living in about 200 communities in the Lacandón jungle.[19]

The Lacandón rainforest is the birthplace of the Zapatista movement.[20] It is the headquarters for the Zapatista army, and most of its inhabitants consider themselves Zapatista civilians. The village of La Realidad—the most important cultural and political center for Zapatistas—is located in the Lacandón forest. This is the area that the government considers a "conflict zone." It is militarized with thousands of troops, dozens of army posts and a large military base in the town of San Quintin.

---

[18]*mestizos*—people of mixed blood (European and indigenous). In Mexico, most people are *mestizos*, so this word is used to designate those who are not Indians.

[19]Xochitl Leyva and Gabriel Ascencio. *Lacandonia al filo del agua* (México: Fondo de Cultura Económica, 1996) pp. 150-151.

[20]The Zapatista National Liberation Army (EZLN) rose up on January 1, 1994. Since then a large social movement has been created to support the Zapatista demands. See Chapter 3 for more information on the Zapatista movement.

The Lacandón rainforest is the most important virgin rainforest preserve in Mexico and it contains a rich biodiversity. For the government of Mexico, however, it also has value as a source of precious tropical lumber, oil and uranium deposits and hydroelectric power. Current struggles will determine the future integrity of the Montes Azules Bioreserve as well as the future of the thousands of indigenous people who live in the rainforest, trying to care for their land and the resources that surround them.

The following pages allow us to follow the life of a family that migrated to the Lacandón rainforest. Their story speaks of their dreams and their struggle to construct a home, a village and a lifestyle. It also tells of the social and political movement that their dream created.

# María's Story[21]

## Ejido Emiliano Zapata
## "Freedom of the Mayan People"

1968. Yes, yes, 1968 was the year. It was in August of 1968 that we walked to the jungle. It was in 1968 that we built our community called Emiliano Zapata in the Lacandón rainforest. Emiliano Zapata is in the municipality of Ocosingo, but now our community is going to be in a new municipality, part of the Zapatistas' autonomous zone. The new municipality is called "Freedom of the Mayan People."

Yes. I can tell you how we walked to the jungle, how we settled the jungle, how we founded this town called Emiliano Zapata and how we organized in the jungle. My husband Nazario was one of the people who founded the communities in the jungle. He was one of

---

[21]Interview with María (not her real name) at *Ejido* Emiliano Zapata, May 12, 1997.

[22]The democratic and independent branch of the Rural Association of Collective Interest (ARIC—Union of Unions).

the people who started the organization *K'ip Tik Talekumtasel,* that later became the ARIC *Democrática-Independiente.*[22]

### My Life on the Plantation

My name is María. I speak Tzotzil, because that's my first language, but I also speak Spanish, Tzeltal and Chol, and I understand a little Tojolabal. I was born on a plantation in the municipality of Sabanilla, which is in northern Chiapas. When I was a child we moved to an *ejido* in the municipality of Huitiupan, a place that is close to the plantation where I was born. We left from that *ejido* in Huitiupan and began our walk to the jungle in 1968, and we founded this community in the jungle called Emiliano Zapata.

My mother was born on the same plantation that I was. My father is from Simojovel, also in northern Chiapas. Both of them are Tzotzil. Life on the plantation was very hard because there was never any rest from work. There was a man who was the overseer, who forced people to work all the time. We even had to work on Sundays, because there was a service we had to provide. We had to give a third of all the firewood we cut to the plantation owner. Another service was to clean his patio. All these "services" were not paid, of course. We had to provide them in exchange for the little piece of land where we planted our corn.

We were very poor. My mother had six children—four sons and two daughters. I'm the oldest. My mother continues to wear her traditional dress. She and my father are quite old. They live with me and my daughter in Emiliano Zapata.

When we moved to the *ejido* in Huitiupan, there was a school and my father sent us there to study. I finished up to third grade. I learned Spanish from my teachers at school. They were federal bilingual education teachers, and they were good teachers. They only spoke Spanish to us. At first, since we only spoke Tzotzil, we couldn't make sense of what they said. But little by little we understood. It was a good experience. We stopped going to school, though, because my father couldn't afford our education any more.[23]

---

[23]Costs of education can include registration fees, uniforms, school supplies, transportation and the loss of the child's hours as a family worker.

# María's Journey

As a child my life was learning to make tortillas, cook the corn-meal and wash clothes. My mother liked to work in the fields with my father, so she would leave very early to go to the fields. When I was about 13 years old, I was in charge of the household. My siblings were boys, so I had to do everything—wash everybody's clothes, prepare the food and clean the house.

We worked the land at the *ejido,* and we continued renting land at the plantation. My father grew potatoes, corn and beans on that land. Mostly, he planted corn. But after a few years, we were asked to plant grass, and the owners put cattle on the grassland. We couldn't work the land after that. The plantation became a cattle ranch and it became more valuable for the owner. He had lots of cattle and good grassland, but we didn't have anywhere to plant corn any more. We lost it. We lost our corn there.

### Looking for Land

I married at a very early age. I was 14 years old. My husband Nazario was from the same community. He was an orphan. His parents died when he was very young. As a child, he had to go look for work elsewhere, so he worked in Simojovel. He worked as a mule-teer, carrying coffee sacks. He supported his brothers and sisters with this work. After a while, he returned to the *ejido* to work in the fields again. Then he was elected by the community to work with the *ejido*'s Agrarian Executive Committee. There was a law called the Agrarian Law that explained how you could start a new *ejido*, how you could get the land and the titles, and how to work on the land. That was his job—to look for land and to deal with the people in the government who could help us.[24]

---

[24] The Agrarian Laws in Article 27 of the 1917 Mexican Constitution gave landless *campesinos* the right to request land communally from the government. This land, called an *ejido*, was communally owned and could be inherited but not sold. In 1992, during the administration of Carlos Salinas, Article 27 was reformed, turning *ejido* land into private property. When *campesinos*, in desperate need for cash, started selling their *ejidos* to corporations and large landowners, the result was the destruction of entire agrarian communities and increased poverty in the countryside. The Zapatistas cite the changes in the Agrarian Law as one of the main reasons for their uprising in 1994.

After some time I already had two daughters, and we thought about looking for land for ourselves. My husband had been working for the committee since he was very young, trying to acquire land for the community. But he hadn't been successful. We never got the papers from the government, so we couldn't get a parcel of land. He had to travel to Tuxtla Gutiérrez all the time to do the paperwork for the *ejido* land. It was there that he met an engineer who was related to his uncle—his mother's younger brother. This engineer worked for the government as an agronomist. His job was to find land for the government to give to the *campesinos*.[25] He was the one who told my husband about the land in the jungle. He asked if we wanted to go there to start a new town, because we didn't own land in Huitiupan. We only rented.

That's how we found this land where we live now. My husband was told in Tuxtla that there was land in the jungle. He went with the engineer to look at the land, and he liked what he saw. Later on he started to get more people to move to the jungle—to the rainforest. We got 40 families together, because the more people there are, the stronger you are to acquire land from the government in Mexico. People were asking my husband, "How is it that you found a person to give you land?" They liked this idea very much. Nobody asked, "Should we go or should we not go?" No. They all said, "We're going!" When my husband came back from his trip to the jungle, and he said, "Yes, it's a good piece of land," people were excited, and more and more people signed up. Those people were the first settlers of this town. So, that's how we came to the jungle in 1968. That was the year we arrived and founded our community.

### *August 1968: The Walk to the Jungle*

"We're going!" my husband said to the family. We got ready and left with him—my father, my mother, my brothers, my little sister, my father-in-law, my brothers-in-law, my two little daughters who

---

[25] In the late 1960s and 1970s, when the Lacandón jungle was open to colonization, the government employed professionals to survey and find state land, or to buy it from private parties for new *ejido* settlements.

were only babies, and myself. We all went in that first trip.

We left on August 1, and we slept that night in Tuxtla Gutiérrez. On the second day, we took the bus to the city of Las Margaritas. That's where the road turns. From Las Margaritas we had a two-hour ride in the back of a truck, and from there we started to walk. The road ended and there was only a mud path to walk on. We walked carrying all our belongings. It was a long way. We started walking at eleven in the morning and we kept walking until six in the evening when we got to a place called Santiago. That's where we slept.

It rained all day, and we had to walk through lots of mud. We walked like that for two days! On the third day, we started at six in the morning, and we got to a place called Agua Velazco. The fourth day we got to a place called San José, a town that's now called Diez de Abril. You could see the jungle from there. Then we kept on walking all the way to Balboa. We arrived at six in the evening, and we rested.

From there we started to walk toward San Quintin. By now we'd been walking for seven days under the rain. We got very tired walking in the mud and through the brush. On August 9, we arrived at the place where we had to cross the Perla River. But there wasn't any bridge—only a little basket big enough for two people hanging from a cable across the river. We had to cross the river like that, hanging in that little basket.

There was only one little footpath that went to Miramar Lake. But our land was on the other side of the lake, so it wasn't any use to us. So the men gave us what they were carrying and started to cut through the brush with their machetes. That's how we went, cutting through the forest. We walked behind them as they cleared the forest ahead of us. If they couldn't cut through the brush, then we had to wait. We walked slowly like that until about three in the afternoon, because there was no road. Finally, we arrived at our land after nine days. Our feet were swollen.

### The Land in the Jungle
We arrived at this land when it was just jungle. It was only brush here, nothing else. There was no house, nothing. My husband and his

brothers built a little hut—not a house—just a little hut made of sticks. We had a little shelf for grinding the corn. When the rain came, and it came all the time, we got soaked. We were here under the rain, in that little hut for 15 days. We suffered.

There were lots of animals when we first got here. You could see deer, jaguars, pacas, monkeys, crocodiles, pheasants, parrots, toucans, macaws, and those animals that you call "tapirs," but we call "elephants" because they are so big. Later on, with all the people that started coming here, the "elephants" went away. They went deeper into the rainforest. They say there are still a lot of them, but that they're far, far away, deep into the jungle, where no people go. I haven't seen them lately, so I don't know. There are still many deer here, but we don't hunt them because it's against the law. Jaguars? I haven't seen them in a long time. Once in a while people say they've seen one. We still see a lot of birds. The parrots fly overhead every evening making lots of noise. There are crocodiles in the rivers, but not at the beaches where we swim.

Later on we built another hut—a little bigger, but not a real house yet—and we moved there. By then the corn was ripe, so we had food to eat. And we also had a few clay pots. We lived like this, with a little food for the two families, and we were alone for about two months.

Then other towns started appearing in the jungle. People were coming and building their little houses. In fact, there are still people coming to the jungle and building their little houses. The Lacandón rainforest is so large that it can hold a lot of people. That's why we came here, because there is a lot of land.

After two months, 20 more people came from the plantation in Huitiupan. Those people flew in a small plane. They say it took them only 60 minutes to get to the jungle—not nine days like it took us! As soon as they came, they started to get organized, and my husband started the paperwork to get the land for them. They all helped with money for my husband's trip to Tuxtla. He had to walk back to Las Margaritas, because like I said, there was no road or bus in those days. After he made two more trips, more people started to arrive. By February, 20 more people came because they wanted to start planting their corn early. More and more people kept coming. By then the government was about to finish the process so we could get the titles to the land.

### The First Land Disputes

In April somebody came looking for us. He said he was the owner of the land, but that wasn't true. He just showed up one day. He said he was a Cuban. We didn't know him. I was in the cornfield harvesting, so the man went by himself to look for my husband. That day, my husband was working on building a new house for us, and that's where the man found him. Later, my husband told me about his conversation with this man. He told me that the man had a gun. In a loud voice, this man told my husband that we couldn't have the land. He said that this was his land and that he was the caretaker of the land. My husband said to him that if this land had had an owner, the fields would have been worked and planted. It wouldn't have been just jungle here if this land had an owner. There had been no house when we got here. There were no worked fields, nothing. We were the ones who cleared the forest when we came.

"No. This is not your land," my husband told this guy. "We have a house now. We have fields. We have our *milpa*—our cornfield. We're getting the papers from the government, because we're the owners now." Well, the man didn't like this, so he left.

Later on, when the engineer who helped us came to our house with our land papers, another "owner" showed up—somebody from San Cristóbal. He said he was the real owner, and that the Cuban man was only his worker. He showed up with his own title papers.

We were sitting at the table in our house, and the engineer handed the *ejido* papers over to my husband. This man pushed the engineer aside and put his own papers on the table in front of my husband. He wanted to take our land, and he started to yell, to push and shove. But my husband didn't lower his voice either. He told him that the land was really ours, and that now we had our title from the government. The man couldn't do anything because his papers were no good. They weren't real. So he left, too.

Rich people kept coming to bother us about the land, saying it was their land. I don't know why. They don't even live here. They are rich men from San Cristóbal or from Ocosingo, or from far away in Mexico City. They have their own lawyers, and they pay them to write titles for land in the rainforest, but they don't live here. Sometimes they had papers that were all wrong, papers for land in the highlands, not in the jungle. They thought they could fool us. None of this is legal, because we have our own legal papers from the government. Eventually those people stopped coming because we became organized to defend our rights. That was later.

### Building a Town

We lived for two or three years without any organization, just learning to survive. Life was very hard in the jungle. There was no store to buy things like soap or salt. We had to go all the way to Ocosingo or Las Margaritas to buy what we needed. It would take us five days to get there, walking on a footpath, among the animals and tall brush.

Around here, the only other settlement was a place we called "The Station." It was run by the forest rangers, whose job it was to take care of the river. Their work was to see how high the river was, to check the water, see if it was still clean—stuff like that. They were here before us. Sometimes they had food that was sent to them, and when they had extra, they sold it to us. They also had little jobs for us to do. They helped us that way.

Then we started to build the town. By now there were a lot of us, and we all organized together. "Let's not be afraid! Let's start working!" we said. That's how we built our town. We never forgot our traditions, our religion, our belief that there is a God. There was always at least one person to lead us in prayer. "I'm the one! I'm going to pray!" somebody would say. All the people were Catholic then. All the people—both Tzotzil and Chol—were united. That's how we got organized. And work that was organized was done right! That's how Ejido Zapata was built.

The women went to work in the fields along with their husbands. In my case, I was the one who worked to support my husband. I had to work more than the others so that my husband could be with the people, organizing.

Before, when we lived and worked on the plantation, it wasn't our land. We were only renting there, so we were constantly having to pay for it. But in Zapata it was our land. This is an *ejido*. It's communal land for 40 families. The whole town—the whole *ejido*— is about 750 hectares. Later on, we divided the land, and each family got 20 hectares.[26] But for two years we organized all the work together, and we started cultivating a larger cornfield together.

As I told you, it was very lonely when we came here. There were a few Lacandón Indians who lived here, but just a few families, really, because this isn't their territory. Most Lacandón people live deeper in the rainforest.[27] José Chambor was a Lacandón Indian who lived with his family here. He became our friend. With his help, my husband and my father built a large *cayuco*—a traditional dug out canoe. Since they'd never made one before, José Chambor taught them. Oh yes! He knew how to make a good *cayuco!* It was beautiful! They used it to fish in the Perla River. There were lots of fish in the river. People used nets to fish, and then they learned to kill the fish with a bow and arrow, just like José Chambor taught them. José Chambor died just this year. He was a good friend. He liked to live down here close to the rivers, so he could fish. José was very good, very kind to us.

The Lacandón still live like in the old days. They wear their traditional dress, which is a white tunic down to their feet. The government likes the Lacandón people a lot. That's because they don't take much land or use too much land to cultivate. They are very good to the land. They take only what they need. They know so much about the forest! On the other hand, the government doesn't like us

---

[26]750 hectares is about 1850 acres, and 20 hectares is about 50 acres.

[27]The Lacandón Mayan Indians are a small group of about 200 hunters and gatherers who have always lived in the rainforest. When the new settlers arrived, the Lacandón Mayans shared with them their great knowledge about living from the rainforest. The friendship and harmony came to an end, however, when some years later the government of Mexico gave the small group of Lacandón Indians the ownership of more than 600,000 *hectares* of rainforest land, and did not give any to thousands of Tzotzil, Tzeltal, Chol, Tojolobal, Zoque and *mestizo* settlers from other states.

very much because we're not like them. We cut lots of brush and forest, and we take up lots of land to plant.

Before long we had more houses. We had lots of cornfields. We planted beans. We raised chickens and pigs. We started to plant all kinds of fruit trees and vegetables. People got organized to plant banana trees, sugar cane, squash—everything! We felt a change in our lives because now we weren't forced to work like we had been on the plantation. We worked as much as we wanted, and we sold as much as we wanted. We sold our products to the forest rangers, to other villagers and to outsiders. We had sows to sell, too, and the pig dealers came all the way from Comitán or Ocosingo—even from San Cristobal. They came in walking and it took them several days to walk back with the pigs. When we sold sows, we bought calves. So, now we had a little money to spend—not much—just a little money. We were growing, becoming richer.

About the third year, we had our first coffee harvest. Some people had planted coffee almost as soon as they arrived, and by the third year the coffee plants started to produce fruit, and we had a good harvest. We still produce coffee in the jungle, and we still sell it. Only now we take it by bus or truck to Ocosingo, but at that time there was no road. In those years we had to walk for a day and a half to sell our coffee, and we had to carry the sacks of coffee on our backs.

We warehoused our coffee in a building owned by the National Indigenous Institute (INI).[28] But they kept it in the warehouse for so long that it rotted with the heat. Or they waited too long to sell it and coffee prices dropped, so we lost our money. Now, we deal with private buyers. Yes, with *coyotes!*[29] We don't always get a good price. The price of coffee depends on so many things beyond our control! But, at least now there's a road to get the coffee out. That's good.

---

[28] The National Indigenous Institute (INI) is a Federal Government institution that works with indigenous people.

[29] The private coffee dealers that buy from the small producers are called *coyotes*. They manipulate the price of coffee, paying the producers as little as possible in order to gain higher profits for themselves.

Soon, there were already about 15 communities on this side of the rainforest: San Quintin, Nueva Providencia, Santa Rosa, San Agustín, La Soledad, Tierra y Libertad, Miguel Alemán and Guerrero. People came mostly from northern Chiapas—from Bachajón, Yajalón, Bochil. There were Tzeltal people from Oxchuc and Abasolo. Here in the jungle we are Tzotzil, Tzeltal, and Chol people. There are also Tojolabal people, and there are Lacandón people. We speak many languages.

### Church Work

Two years after we got to Zapata, a priest showed up. His name was Vicente. There was a nun as well, Sister Mary. There was also a lay Christian Brother who we called Brother Javier. Father Vicente led us in worship. He trained catechists and Delegates of the Word,[30] those we call *"mayordomos."*[31] He helped to build the church. Sister Mary helped with all the church work.

Javier was the composer of our community. He wrote our official *ejido* song. It's a beautiful song about how the community was founded. When he finished writing it, he called everybody in the community together and sang it. The community listened to it and then we all sang it. We all learned that song! He wrote other hymns, too. He left us with a lot of them. He worked with us like that for five years. When he left, he gave us all his compositions, all his hymns and the *ejido* song. We still have all of it. I don't know where Javier went, but we heard that Father Vicente and Sister Mary went to India. They even sent us their greetings all the way from there! You get attached to good people. You remember them.

---

[30] Delegates of the Words are Catholic lay leaders trained to official liturgies in the absence of a priest.

[31] In the traditional Mayan system in the highlands, the *mayordomos* are those who are in charge of organizing the religious feast days and caring for the religious icons called *santos*. This system was transferred to the jungle and "modernized." Because of the lack of clergy and the distance between communities, *mayordomos*, catechists and Delegates of the Word became the spiritual leaders of the communities. Their work was to preach the Gospel, to organize and to build unity among the communities.

## *Political Work*

After a while, our work of building the town was done. About that time, the government started to work in the area where the Lacandón people live, in the Montes Azules Bio-Reserve area. We were told that all the people from the communities, including our Ejido Zapata, were going to be thrown off the land. They were saying that it was part of the reserve. But that's not true. Our communities aren't inside the reserve.

We were very well organized, because we had learned about politics. In the same year that the priest came, another man came into our communities. His name was Jaime, and his wife's name was Alma Rosa. She was the one who taught us about politics—about the laws, about the Agrarian Reform, the articles of the Constitution, all of that. We had workshops in the communities about how we could speak up and defend our rights. We learned that if somebody wanted to take our land we had to defend ourselves. We learned what to do and what to say to defend our land. My husband already knew all of this. He had lots of experience from his previous work. So I was able to help teach the classes.

There was also another teacher. He was an anthropologist. He gave classes too. That's where more people learned to read—those who wanted to study, at least. He was good. He prepared the community teachers. He taught them himself. When he saw that they had learned, he sent them to work in the communities. The teachers got paid a little salary. It wasn't much. It was just a stipend to help them out a little. The children learned a lot then, because before this, the children had no schooling at all.

My husband continued helping other communities with his work on the Agrarian Committee in the rainforest. He saw that the communities couldn't do everything by themselves. How were they going to go to Tuxtla to talk with the authorities there? They didn't know how. So my husband went to talk for them. All the communities were now part of the organization of *ejidos*. We had a lot of neighbors, and we knew and helped each other. We felt that now there was more friendship. We didn't feel like we were alone anymore. It was nice to live like that.

My husband kept organizing and helping communities to get their land titles. He helped the *ejido* called Nueva Providencia get its title. And he helped another *ejido*, Miguel Hidalgo, too. We named our towns with good names. "What shall we call our town?" people would say. "You should call it Miguel Hidalgo after our Independence hero," my husband said. Another *ejido,* they named La Libertad, which means freedom.

There were already a lot of us in Zapata. The first settlers had a lot of children. They found another piece of land behind the hills, and they said, "We're going to divide our town. Half of us will go there, and half of us will stay here." It was a nice piece of land. They started to work, and they built a new town. So, the town of Zapata was divided in two.

Well, the government always notices these things. The government didn't want people to settle in the Montes Azules Reserve, and it didn't want more people in the rainforest, because people cut lots of brush. That's what the government told us. My husband was the one who talked with the government the most. He had to defend our rights.

### *K'ip Tik Talekumtasel*

Later on, there were also plantations in the jungle—not where we have our land, but farther away. It was those rich people I told you about who owned them. They did the same thing again. They cleared out the forest to plant grass for cattle. But in some places they had coffee. Workers were being exploited on the plantations, and my husband decided to try to help them.

"Work for yourselves," he told them. "Don't work for others, and don't let them abuse you." He told the workers to become members of the organization called *"K'ip Tik Talekumtasel,"* which is a Tzeltal name that means, "The strength of the organization is for our welfare." That's why the plantation owners hated him.

The plantation owners called the army—10 soldiers—to throw the workers out. The workers decided not to wait, and they went to ask the soldiers what they wanted. The soldiers didn't even answer. They just pulled their guns and started to shoot. When the workers saw that the bullets were coming at them, they started shooting too. There was a shoot out. So, the plantation owners hated my husband even more.

## *My Husband*

On a Monday around noon, my husband was working in the *acagual*.[32] That day he was cutting brush. He was almost done with his work. Two people I'd never seen before came to the house to look for him around nine in the morning. I thought that perhaps my husband knew them, so I welcomed them. I was getting ready to go over to where he was working, but because my child was little I didn't want to go. So, I told them, "Oh, I was going to take my husband his lunch, but why don't you take it to him so I won't have to leave my child alone in the house."

My husband usually got home late from working in the fields, but that night he didn't make it back. The next morning I was still waiting. I sent my daughter to look for him in the *acagual*. She said she looked all over. About three in the afternoon, we all went to look for him. We went to the cattle yard, but didn't find him there. Other people found him on the road. He was dead.

My husband was killed that night with a machete. I don't know really who killed him. The truth is, I don't know. I think he was killed because he worked for the people. There were political problems already. The government was already getting involved in our politics, and the plantation owners were angry at my husband because he was organizing the workers. I think the people who killed him were "white guards." You see, my husband had organized the people, and people were very united because of him. He knew how to work.

My husband was killed in 1977, and people were paralyzed after he died. The organization my husband founded, the *K'ip Tik Talekumtasel*, fell apart when somebody else started to lead it. That's when the divisions and the problems started. By 1983, there was a crisis in the organization and some people were expelled from it.

---

[32] *acagual*—the low underbrush land, outside of the rainforest.

## *Work as a Catechist*

After my husband was killed, I started working as a catechist. I was also working in political organizing with men and women. It seemed to me that there were no leaders—that the people had been abandoned. That's why I started to work as a catechist.

When I was a child living at the plantation, I couldn't speak Tzeltal, because only Tzotzil and Chol was spoken there. But here in the jungle, many communities speak Tzeltal. I was a teacher for some time, working with women. I heard them talk in Tzeltal and so I learned to speak. I learned fast. Then, when I worked as a catechist, I learned even more. It's not difficult for me to speak Tzeltal.

When I was a catechist and an organizer, we helped women with the cooperatives and we worked cultivating beans. After that we had a store. That one still exists. The women who were learning with us there manage the store now. I still work with the Church. I do what I can.

## *Mayan Culture*

I worked a lot as a catechist. We started a new kind of work called "The Mayan Culture." We learned about the old Mayan culture, how people lived and cultivated in the old times. *Ay*, and we learned that we are Mayans. We didn't know this before, you see. We always knew we were Indians, that we were Tzeltales, or Tzotziles, or Choles, or Tojolabales. But we didn't know the word, *Maya*. We didn't know we were Mayans. That opened our eyes and our ears. We learned about how the old Mayans started their civilization. We learned that we are the same as them. Now I have seen all the old places of the Mayans. We know it very well now, how the ancient Mayans lived. We learned how they cultivated. Some of the food they ate was different, but some food was the same as the food we eat now.

There is a book called the *Popol Vuh* that talks about where our people came from. In this book we read that we are made of *masa*, or corn dough. Yes, yes, we are *masa*. People know this. Now, the other Scriptures, they talk about other people, people from other nations. For example, in the Bible it says that all people were created by God and came from Adam and Eve. We know this. We believe this—that we were created by God. The *Popol Vuh* tells us that God created people not only over there in those other nations, but that God created people here too, and that we are made of *masa*. So, we believe what it says in the Bible—that we were created by God—but we also believe that we are made of *masa*. This is the awareness that our people have. We like it because that belief has remained. It's still here. It is our life. The children learn this, too.

We also learned from the work with Mayan Culture that we should not cut down the forest. So now we've changed, and we don't cut the forest. "The forest is good," the *campesinos* say, "because it is our life." So, now we only cut in the *acaguales*, which is the short brush. We don't cut in the tall forest. We don't cut in the high hills, we only cut in the low hills and short brush, so we don't hurt the trees. There are still a lot of trees in the rainforest—many, many trees. The trees are also in the hearts of the *campesinos*. We don't cut trees down anymore. Now we are like the Lacandón Indians. Like them, we know that the forest is our life. We don't want anybody coming and cutting our forest. We won't allow this anymore.

In our communities, the children speak many languages. The Tzotzil children speak Tzotzil, but they also speak Spanish, Chol and Tzeltal. They meet different people, so they learn. Let's say a person speaks Chol. The child hears the person and learns it. Or a child listens when a person speaks Tzeltal, and the child just understands. That's how it works.

### Life in Ejido Emiliano Zapata

As I told you, the organization my husband started was called *K'ip Tik Talekumtasel*, "The strength of the organization is for our good." That is what it was called in his time. It was the Union of Unions that was formed in 1969, when the *ejido* was still new. My husband was one of the people who started it. It's the same organization that became the ARIC, and in 1994 it became ARIC *Independiente y Democrática.*

Throughout the 1970s we worked with ARIC. By 1978 the work we were doing was getting into people's consciences. Then it entered into their hearts. But, as I told you, in the early 1980s there were many problems with the organization. Then, in 1994, the ARIC divided into two after the Zapatista uprising. It was because people were bringing in government politics from the office in Ocosingo. In other words, it was really the government that was running ARIC, not the people. That was bad, and that's when it divided. The people who were receiving salaries from the government stayed with the old organization, and the ones without salary separated and started the ARIC *Democrática-Independiente*. The government group is called the ARIC *Oficial,* and the group that is managed by the *campesinos*, where people organize, is the ARIC *Independiente*. ARIC *Independiente* is the one that agrees with the Zapatistas' demands.[33]

We started working with the Zapatistas in recent years. At first it was very clandestine. We had contact with them early on, before they were called Zapatistas. Only a few people met with them, underground, little by little. By 1993 everybody knew. Now most people in the *ejido* belong to ARIC *Independiente*, and we are part of the Zapatista's civilian base of support.

There are those who don't want to know anything. It's as if they were blind and deaf. There's a small group of Jehovah's Witnesses, for example, who don't want anything to do with this. They're against it. But they live here in the community, and they have to be part of the community. Sometimes they become smart, especially when they see our strength. Then they start getting close to us, little by little.

Our life has changed a lot since 1994. Now women participate in the work. Before 1994, most women didn't participate. Now there are delegates, secretaries who see what kind of work needs to be done. And now women have our own organizations. We work on our own in the store. We have our meetings by themselves. We elect our representatives on our own—a secretary, and a treasurer to look after the money.

---

[33] ARIC Oficial is the smaller of the two factions. It has collaborated with government policies, including counterinsurgency policies, in the rainforest area.

### San Quintin Military Base

We have lots of problems now because the military base is here next to us in the town of San Quintin. Most people in San Quintin are members of the government party, the PRI. Only a road separates the two towns. There are many problems with the army—prostitution, for instance. And we can't go to the fields without being harassed by soldiers. They don't leave us alone. When the women of our community see that the soldiers are misbehaving, we complain. Because we don't think that prostitution is good. That's where we organize with a strong voice, because we don't want prostitution to come into Zapata. The people are resolute. We don't want the soldiers to come to our community. They cannot come with their weapons. If they are unarmed they can come in. But we don't want war.

In 1994, right after the Zapatista uprising, we had to run. Our town was bombed, and we were afraid. People ran to the mountains. We were there for three days without food. We said to each other, "The children are going to die here. It would be better to die with full stomachs in our homes, and not here in the forest without food. We are going to return, no matter what happens. We are going to fight with our people. We are ready to die with our people." But we didn't die. We returned to our town because of the children.

We have a law against alcohol. There are still people who drink, but it's against the law here. It's the women who worked more on this policy, because men get messed up when they drink. So things are changing. Women's eyes are more open now. Young women are moving along, too, because the experience of the mother becomes the experience of the daughter. Even the little girls know how to take care of themselves.

We have a community education project that we manage ourselves. It's not from the federal government. No, it's our project. We have teachers who are members of our organization and who are trained with community support. We have six community teachers who teach first to sixth grade. The children are learning a lot. There are about 20 children in each class. We've had community teachers for two years now. We used to have government teachers, bilingual education teachers. That was a problem because there were teachers who came from other areas who didn't understand our traditions, our way of life. Other teachers were against our politics, and against our way of organizing.

People here like to have *fiestas*. We're used to our traditions. We don't want to abandon our traditions, our customs. For example, every year on August 9, we have a big party to celebrate the founding of the community. The little ones grow up hearing the history of the Ejido Emiliano Zapata. We also celebrate Emiliano Zapata's birthday, and other holidays that are important to us.

The health promoters were trained when the international aid came in 1994, right after the uprising. At that time the international doctors came here to help. They brought lots of medicine and they trained our health promoters. The big trucks with medicine and aid from the international and national solidarity parked on the other side of Perla River and crossed the medicines on the *cayucos*—carved wooden canoes. *Cayuco* after *cayuco* was filled with aid and medicines. So, for three years we had good medicine. Now the medicine has almost run out. We have very good health promoters, but they don't have much medicine to work with now.

There are a lot of ailments here because we are very poor. There is a lot of malnutrition among the children. Last year there was a cholera epidemic here. My grandson got very sick, and we thought he was going to die. He was only a baby then. It's hard for us since we don't have medicine, and we're not treated well in the government clinics. I think that's because they say we are Zapatistas. When people from San Quintin go to the clinic, they get good treatment.

On May 10 of this year of 1997, on Mother's Day, we had a huge march of about three thousand people who came from all the communities close by. It was a march against the army base in San Quintin. Also the march was against the state government because it insists on having its own type of municipality here. We don't want that. The government wants a municipality where it can control us.

We don't want that. We want to be independent. We want to be an autonomous municipality called, "Freedom of the Mayan People."[34]

---

[34] As communities returned from hiding and regrouped after the army offensive of February 1995, the Zapatista rebels began to encourage the formation of "autonomous communities" which would govern themselves and accept no assistance from the government. See Chapters 3-5 for more information about autonomous communities.

Author's postscript: By 1998, the Zapatistas had declared the area around Ejido Emiliano Zapata an autonomous municipality called Libertad de los Pueblos Mayas or "Freedom for the Mayan People." The capital of the municipality under this Zapatista system is Santa Rosa El Copán. In 1999, however, the Chiapas State government began dividing large official municipalities and creating new ones. According to the government, Ejido Emiliano Zapata is now in the municipality of San Quintin with the capital in the town of San Quintin just a few miles from Emiliano Zapata.

In 1997, when I visited Ejido Emiliano Zapata, the military base in San Quintin was still under construction, and the people of Emiliano Zapata were very concerned about it. The base was finished in 1998 and is now one of the largest military bases in Chiapas. Maria and her family live almost next door to it. In recent years the situation has worsened for the people of the rainforest as militarization has increased, paramilitary groups have been formed and government policies of harassment and intimidation against Zapatista municipalities has intensified.

Since 1999, serious conflicts have also occurred in rainforest communities like Amador Hernández as people have opposed the construction of roads through their villages. The government claims that these roads are for the development of tourism, but community people suspect that they are for the transportation of troops. In early 2000—after the rainforest had been completely encircled by roads—large numbers of soldiers were sent to the region in a so-called "reforestation" project. Again, community members have protested this kind of excuse for increasing army presence. Farmers continue to be blamed for the destruction of the rainforest, and protection of the environment is often used as a pretext for evicting settlers—most of them Zapatista civilians.

The people who live in the rainforest continue to organize in *campesino* groups and as Zapatista civilians. They continue to hold claim to their land, and they insist on defending their territory and their dream against outside interference. María's family is still living in Ejido Emiliano Zapata. It is a hard life—one of resistance, organization and struggle.

✳

# TWO

# San Cristóbal de las Casas:
# A City of Contrasts

© Xunka' López Díaz

# IN EVERY CORNER

In every corner you see me
every day.
From so much seeing me,
you stop seeing me.
      In every corner you see me
      and you no longer see me
      because you don't want to see me.
You ignore me,
you pass me by.
I am there and you act as if I weren't there.
When I talk to you
      you don't listen
      you don't answer
      you walk away.
I am there
in every corner of the city,
sitting on the sidewalk
with a child tied to my back
and another one playing by my side.
      I am there
      Wearing a multicolor
      flowered blouse,
      woolen skirt,
      bare feet.
            I am there
            selling dolls with ski-masked faces,
            with rifles in hand,
            with wooden horses.
            And you,
            only pass me by.
I wonder:
If I myself had
      a ski-masked face
      and rifle in hand,
            what then
            would you do?
                  would you talk to me then?
                  would you just pass me by?

*—Teresa Ortiz*

# A CITY OF CONTRASTS

As I sit in one of the benches at *el parque*—the central park of San Cristóbal de las Casas, Chiapas—a couple of Tzotzil girls approach me, trying to convince me to buy their handwoven friendship bracelets. My "no thank yous" are to no avail. They are determined to make a sale. If I'm not interested in the bracelets, they pull handmade Zapatista dolls out of their bags. Still not interested? How about a clay Chamula doll? Or a clay whistle in the shape of a strange animal? It might be a dog or a frog, I'm not sure. Or how about a *gallinita*—a woven potholder in the shape of a hen? I know it was made in Guatemala, but the girls insist they made it themselves, or that their mother did, or that it was made by their poor neighbor woman in *La Hormiga*[1] who—according to the girls—is too old to come to the park to sell.

Although my graying hair always makes me look like a *guerita*— a blondie—I finally convince them that I am not a foreigner, that I live in San Cristóbal, that I have seen their wares a hundred times before, and that I am definitely not interested in buying. I tell them to try the *gringos* sitting on the next bench. They run towards them like a couple of squirrels, talking at the same time, fighting with each other to make the first sale. Standing by the *gringos* and leaning on the iron fence railing, a group of punk-looking San Cristóbal teenagers laugh at the girls.

## Tourists, Street Children and Hippies

This is a city of many contrasts, and you can see them all if you are in *el parque*. On any given day, and especially in the summer, you can see an array of tourists from different countries, speaking many different languages. Some have dreadlocks and carry backpacks. Others wear shorts and carry cameras. Some are in small groups, and others arrive as a pack in the huge buses that follow the "Mayan Route"—the route that takes tourists to Mayan archaeological sites,

---

[1] *La Hormiga*, a neighborhood on a hillside overlooking San Cristóbal, is populated by Mayan Tzotzil people, the majority of whom are evangelical Protestants who have been expelled from the Municipality of San Juan Chamula.

Indian markets, historical landmarks, colonial cities and fancy beach resorts. They start in Chiapas and go to the Yucatán Peninsula, finishing up in Cancún.

There are many Mexican tourists in *el parque* as well, particularly during the traditional Mexican holiday seasons of Easter and Christmas. Upper-middle-class Mexicans who want to go back to their roots during their vacation time often choose to visit indigenous and colonial cities like San Cristóbal. Here, they search for their true Mexican heritage and take a personal trip back into their nation's history. Other visitors include young college students, alternative political activists and Zapatista sympathizers. They fill up the city whenever there are forums or events, arriving alone or in small groups to work as peace campers, human rights observers or accompaniers.[2] San Cristóbal is a stop on the way to their final destinations, which are the communities in *Las Cañadas*, the highlands or the rainforest.

Many local folks live off these tourists: the Tzotzil girls who run after the tourists selling candy or gum, Zapatista dolls or friendship bracelets; the boys who sell *La Jornada* and other newspapers or shine shoes; and their mothers who sit on nearby corners or walk through the park selling their handiwork.

If you spend time in the artisan markets of Santo Domingo Park, San Francisco Park and Insurgentes Street, you will find the people known locally as "the hippies." They are artisans, jewelry makers, musicians, other bohemians and long-hairs, and the local teenagers who try to imitate them by hanging out and acting cool. These "hippie" artisans have been coming to San Cristóbal since the sixties, traveling on a different kind of Mayan Route—the route of young backpackers in search of alternative lifestyles and mind-altering substances. Their route takes them from the beaches of Oaxaca, to the Chiapas highlands, to Palenque and the rain forest, and into Guatemala. San Cristóbal is a stop—long or short—on their journey.

---

[2]Peace campers are physically present in rural communities that are at risk of being invaded or harassed by the army. They are there to deter and/or be witnesses to any human rights violations that may occur. "Accompaniers" perform a similar function with individuals at risk.

# SAN CRISTÓBAL DE LAS CASAS

Tuxla Gutiérrez

*The Highlands*

San Cristóbal de las Casas

### *Middle-Class* Coletos, Auténticos *and Non-*coletos

Nicely dressed Mexican businessmen and their professional or stay-at-home wives are also present in San Cristóbal. You can see them going for a stroll in the park, sitting on park benches or in the nearby cafés or bars, working in government offices or professional firms, or managing banks or department stores. They are the local middle-class society, those who call themselves *coletos*. The term *coleto*—which means literally "pony tail" and refers to the way the Spanish colonizers wore their hair in the 17th century—is merely the term that designates those people born and raised in San Cristóbal. Many upper-class, conservative people, however, like to call themselves *auténticos coletos,* which suggests that they, and they only, are the genuine descendants of the first Spanish settlers, and that as such, they have a greater right to make decisions that affect San Cristóbal life.[3] Too late for that. San Cristóbal is no longer Ciudad Real, the conservative and provincial highland capital of colonial Chiapas, where the descendants of the first European settlers ruled over Indians and land. San Cristóbal has changed tremendously in the twentieth century, and the events of the last decade have ensured that it has changed forever.

There are other middle-class professionals who reside in San Cristóbal and have helped to shape its new face. They are from other parts of Mexico—Mexico City in particular—or from other countries. Some of them were born in San Cristóbal, but still don't call themselves *coletos.* They are artists and artisans. They are business people who run hotels, bars, cafés, restaurants, and other tourist related services. They are anthropologists, environmentalists and natural science professionals working in academic institutions. They are service professionals working in non-governmental organizations, assisting indigenous cooperatives and facilitating development projects throughout Chiapas. Most of the San Cristóbal non-*coleto* residents are liberals, and many of them are leftists and social activ-

---

[3]*Auténticos coletos* are generally opposed to the Zapatistas and to any negotiations with them. They feel that San Cristóbal has fallen into decadence, and blame the Catholic Church of Samuel Ruíz, foreigners and the indigenous.

ists involved in the struggle for civil rights, democratic change and social justice. They are part of the movement that has swept through Mexico in the final decades of the 20th century, culminating in Chiapas with the emergence of the Zapatista movement in 1994. Many middle-class non-*coleto* residents of San Cristóbal are full supporters of the Zapatista movement. (It would be fair to say that there is also a segment of *coleto* society who supports this movement.)

**Working-Class *Coletos***

Then, there are the hidden wheels that move San Cristóbal: the sellers in shops and markets, the drivers of taxis and buses, the food vendors in parks and city corners, the construction workers, the mechanics and the small service providers. These are really the people that make San Cristóbal what it is. They are the working-class *coletos* and the indigenous Mayans.

The working-class *coletos*, like the upper-middle-class *auténticos*, have also been San Cristóbal natives for many generations, and many of them have Spanish ancestry dating all the way back to the 16th and 17th centuries. However, these *coletos* are not white-skinned descendants of Europeans. They are the mixed-blood descendants of the Indians who, together with the Spanish colonizers, helped populate the city after it was founded in 1528.

At that time, Ciudad Real—as San Cristóbal was called then—was established in Tzotzil Chamula territory in the valley of Jovel. The Spanish *conquistadores* pushed the Tzotzil and Chamula Indians back to their ancestral capital—now called San Juan Chamula—and to the surrounding mountainous territory. In order to subdue the local Tzotzil and Tzeltal highland Indians, they brought their own "friendly" Indians with them—the Mexicanos and Tlaxcaltecas from the central valley of Mexico. Spanish families settled in the central part of Ciudad Real, surrounded and protected by friendly Indian settlements. In the 17th century, more settlements were created and populated by other groups of "friendly" Indians.[4] Even in those early colonial times, San Cristóbal was a city of many cultures and many languages, with the presence of the Spanish, the Chiapas highland Mayans, Guatemalan Mayans, and Indians from central Mexico. Intermarriage between the Spanish and Indians became common—as it was throughout Mexico—and resulted in racially-mixed children who were called *mestizos*.[5] Each settlement—or *barrio*—acquired a specific character and culture of its own, characterized by unique handicrafts, trades and *fiestas*. In *Cuxtitali*, for example, the Quiché became pork butchers, while the *Barrio of Guadalupe* settlers became leather-work artisans who have taken the December 12 feast day of Our Lady of Guadalupe as their town's special feast day. The descendants of these mixed-blood people are the present day working-class *coletos*, and their cultural traditions and religious celebrations continue even today. They are religious, enterprising and very hard working people. Yet, despite their indigenous heritage, the working-class *coletos* do not consider themselves Indians.[6]

The history of colonization by the Spanish left its imprint on the culture and ideology of San Cristóbal. In 1773 its name was changed from Ciudad Real to San Cristóbal de las Casas in honor of both patron Saint Christopher and Fray Bartolomé de las Casas. Bartolomé de las Casas was a 16th century monk and ardent defender of indigenous rights. As a result of his advocacy efforts, Pope Paul III issued

---

[4]The history of San Cristóbal *barrios* has been documented by Andrés Aubry in *San Cristóbal de las Casas: su historia urbana demográfica y monumental 1528-1990* (1991).

[5]Documents and lithographs at the Museum of History in Santo Domingo Convent in San Cristóbal de las Casas provide us with descriptions of various racial mixtures which determined a person's place in the colonial social strata. The Spanish colonizers were at the top of the social scale, followed by the Spanish born in America who were called *criollos*. *Mestizos* occupied a lower rank, followed by *indios* (Indians), *mulatos* (children of African and Spanish) and so on.

[6]*Mujeres de Tierra Fría: conversaciones con las coletas* by Diana Rus (Universidad de Ciencias y Artes del Estado de Chiapas, 1997) is a wonderful work of testimonies of *coleta* women that provides us with an in-depth analysis of the complexities of life for the non-Indian San Cristóbal women.

his 1537 letter, *Sublimus Deus*, calling for better treatment of the Indians. In spite of these efforts, however, San Cristóbal remained a highly conservative, deeply religious and even racist town over the years. Even as late as the 20th century, Tzotzil people from Chamula and Zinacantán and Tzeltal people from surrounding highland villages were not allowed to live in San Cristóbal. When they came to town to sell their produce, they couldn't walk on the sidewalks, and they were not allowed to remain in San Cristóbal overnight. Often, the *coletos* bought Indian wares for less than their real value on the outskirts of town and then resold them for a profit in San Cristóbal. The *coletos* justified cheating the *"inditos"*—as they called them—by saying that they lived in a barter economy and did not appreciate the value of money, while the city residents worked extremely hard to make a living.

Today, there are still working-class *coletos* who continue to think of themselves as superior to the highland Indians, even if their skin color and their ancestry are the same. They still use pejorative names such as *"indito"* or *"chamulita"* when referring to the Tzotzil and Tzeltal people. They still argue that indigenous people are "lazy" or "unmotivated," that they drink too much, and that this is the reason they remain poor. These *coletos* do not accept the argument that indigenous people have been exploited since the arrival of the Spanish, or that all non-Indian residents of San Cristóbal are direct beneficiaries of this exploitation.

However, more and more *coletos* are changing their attitudes and beliefs. The ideological and religious revolution that swept through the *Las Cañadas* and rainforest areas of Chiapas in the 1970s, accompanied by the liberation theology of the Diocese of San Cristóbal and Bishop Samuel Ruíz, also transformed the lives of many people in conservative San Cristóbal. Many *coletos* who were members of the diocese were organized by neighborhoods into Christian base communities, in the same way that the indigenous people organized in their villages. Through discussions held in these Bible-study groups, many working-class *coletos* came to understand their own personal oppression as poor *mestizos*. But even more importantly, they came to understand that they had been the oppressors of their indigenous brothers and sisters. In addition to their work with the Church, these Catholic *coletos* have organized politically into grassroots citizen groups that are active in opposition political parties. Together they protest unjust government policies and demand peace, democracy and human rights. And they give their full support to the indigenous Zapatistas.[7]

## Los Expulsados

The largest and most important segment of the working-class poor of San Cristóbal are the Mayan Tzotzil people living in the outskirts of the city, in the hills of *La Hormiga, Nueva Esperanza* and other marginal neighborhoods. These Tzotzil people began to arrive in San Cristóbal in the early 1970s. They are mostly evangelical Protestants who were expelled from the municipality of San Juan Chamula by their neighbors, the so-called "traditionalists," who are led by the local political bosses called *caciques*.[8]

The history of the Chamula expulsions is a complex one that has lasted 30 years and affected 15,000 to 30,000 Mayans—primarily evangelical Protestants[9]—who are currently living in marginal urban areas and makeshift rural settlements. It is a history of violence, religious intolerance, political corruption, economic interests and land ownership conflicts. Although the apparent justification for the expulsion of evangelical Tzotziles by "traditionalist" Tzotziles

---

[7]Two examples of progressive *coleto-mestizo* groups are BACOSAN (Barrios and Neighborhoods of San Cristóbal) and CIUSPAZ (San Cristóbal Citizens for Peace).

[8]In Chiapas, *Caciques* are local community indigenous political bosses, usually allied to the government and to the non-Indian economic elites. They are often active members of the PRI party and hold important political positions gotten, not through free elections, but by corrupt political alliances with state government officials. They hold political and economic power, and maintain it by force. Many times *caciques* are the children and grandchildren of *caciques*.

[9]According to Edras Alonso González in *San Juan Chamula: persecución de indígenas evangélicos* (Editorial Alfa y Omega, 1995), 34,000 indigenous Tzotzil evangelicals have been expelled from San Juan Chamula and other highlands municipalities. Other sources say that 15,000-25,000 of the expelled are living in San Cristóbal and the municipality of Teopisca.

from Chamula and other towns has been religious and ethnic purity, the root causes of the conflict are primarily political and economic.[10] To analyze every dimension of the conflict and the expulsions would take an entire book. I discuss it briefly here, only in order to introduce the Mayan women of San Cristóbal whose voices will be heard in the upcoming interviews.

It is important to point out that Mayan people are deeply religious, whether they are evangelical Protestants, liberation theology Catholics, syncretic traditionalists,[11] or Mayan spiritual leaders who practice ancient pre-Colombian rituals. The spirituality of the Mayan people is expressed in their daily lives. In indigenous communities, Mayan people bless the seed before they plant it, and they thank the corn for giving them nourishment before the harvest. Mother Earth is sacred, and the farmer asks her permission to till. Everything that surrounds us is also sacred: the sun, the moon and the stars in the heavens; the water in rivers and lakes; the mountains and valleys; the plants, the animals and the people on earth. For the Mayan people, everything and everybody deserves our respect. Mayan people use the word "respect" when they talk about this special relationship they have with nature. Worship is the ritualized demonstration of respect for the sacredness of it all—for the *Corazón del Cielo-Corazón de la Tierra,* the male-female deity found in nature and the heavens that is both Father God and Mother Earth.

Mayan spirituality has survived and adapted throughout history. The Catholic evangelization of the 16th century aided, accompanied and sometimes mitigated the violence of the Spanish military invasion. It did not completely eradicate the ancient spirituality, however. Newly converted Christian Indians adapted their own rituals and be-

---

[10]"Religious Intolerance and Discrimination in San Juan Chamula," *Conquest Continued, Disregard for Human and Indigenous Rights in the Mexican State of Chiapas,* Minnesota Lawyers International Human Rights Committee Report, August 1992, pp. 51-58.
[11]Religious syncretism is a combination of various beliefs and religious practices into a new one. In this case, it is the combination of Catholicism with Mayan spiritual beliefs. This syncretic religion is called *tradicionalista* or *costumbrista* in Spanish.

liefs to the rituals and theology of Catholicism, producing the deeply spiritual and very ritualistic form of Catholicism practiced in indigenous communities today. The Catholicism practiced by poor *mestizos* in Mexico is also, in some ways, the result of this mixture of Indian spirituality and Catholicism. Our Lady of Guadalupe—the Mexican Indian mother of Jesus—for example, is the most important and venerated symbol of both Catholicism and Mexican national identity.

San Juan Chamula is an extremely conservative and traditionalist Mayan Tzotzil town in the highlands of Chiapas, where this form of religious syncretism has been practiced since colonial times. For the Tzotzil people there, San Juan Chamula is a most sacred place, the center of the universe. The entrance to Chamula is marked by the sky-blue crosses that are found in all sacred Mayan sites in the highlands of Chiapas. In Chamula, as well as in other Mayan Tzotzil villages of the highlands, the rituals involve the use of candles, incense, ritual drinking of alcoholic beverages and of sugar-water, and chanting in Tzotzil. But this kind of deeply spiritual ritual has been corrupted in San Juan Chamula by the partisan politics and economic interests of a small powerful group of Indian *caciques* who are supported by the official PRI party government.

Traditionally, Mayan citizens do not vote. Rather, they choose their political authorities by consensus in public forums or assemblies in which all members of the community participate and have a voice. The local political leader who then is chosen becomes, a servant of the community. This system has been changed and corrupted in many highland communities since the 1950s, when the influence and imposition of the federal and state governments became stronger. At that time, the system of electing authorities was imposed on communities by the PRI with the support of powerful state politicians and members of the non-Indian economic elite. In the end, political posts were given out as prizes to the indigenous leaders who could keep their communities from rebelling or demanding their rights. San Juan Chamula, now a predominantly PRI municipality, is the best example of a case where the old Mayan system of decision-making by consensus has been corrupted by the official PRI party, and where elected positions have been held by powerful and corrupt *caciques.*

In Chamula, the *caciques* have accumulated economic power. They have used the traditionalist religion for their personal commercial benefit by selling bootleg liquor and candles, and by selling concessions to soda companies like Coca Cola and Pepsi Cola, which have replaced the traditional sugar-water. They have also used their political positions to obtain personal benefits from government subsidies, allowing them to accumulate land and wealth.

When the first Protestant conversions of indigenous people in the highlands started to take place in the 1960s—first with the work of the Presbyterian church, and later with the proselytizing campaigns of fundamentalist and pentecostal missionaries—the "traditionalist" *caciques* felt that their economic and political power was at stake. The newly converted Christians took to their new religion with a great passion. They didn't drink or spend their money on candles or rituals. They believed in working hard, and they demanded action against corrupt practices. Many of them became members of opposition political parties. In short, they challenged the political and economic interests of the local Indian elite. As a result, the indigenous evangelicals were expelled from the villages by the *caciques* and their traditionalist followers. The expulsions were extremely violent. People were attacked physically and their homes were burned.[12]

In the early 1970s the indigenous evangelicals who were expelled from Chamula arrived in San Cristóbal de las Casas and began living in makeshift neighborhoods on the mountainsides that surround the city. As one might imagine, the newly arrived Indians were not exactly welcomed with open arms. In fact, they faced discrimination and mistreatment at the hands of most of the long-term residents of the city. Ironically, they found an ally in the Catholic Church of Bishop Samuel Ruíz, which defended their human rights despite the fact that they were Protestants. In return, the expelled Chamula Indians have become supporters of the diocese. In 1995,

---

[12]Esdras Alonso González, *San Juan Chamula: Persecución de indígenas evangélicos,* Editorial Alfa y Omega, 1995.

when a group of *auténticos* waged an attack on Samuel Ruíz for his role in mediating the peace talks between the Zapatistas and the Mexican government, the expelled evangelicals—together with other San Cristóbal citizens—formed a human chain around the San Cristóbal Cathedral to protect the Bishop.

The expelled Tzotzils joined unions and social organizations, as well as opposition political parties like the left of center PRD and the conservative PAN.[13] Today the Tzotzil Chamulas are an important economic and social segment of the San Cristóbal population. The majority are extremely poor, and yet many of them have organized to run the markets and several of the taxi cooperatives.

The arrival of the expelled Tzotzils marked the beginning of great change for San Cristóbal. The old colonial and provincial city—the racist town where Indians were not allowed to stay the night—changed dramatically and became a true multi-cultural city. Then, on January 1, 1994, San Cristóbal was taken over by a group of Mayan campesinos who called themselves Zapatistas. This moment marked the beginning of even more dramatic changes for San Cristóbal and for Chiapas.

But, as the following testimonies of Mayan women indicate, it's still not easy to be a poor Indian woman in San Cristóbal. The lives of the women interviewed in this chapter are similar to those of thousands of indigenous women living in the city in that they are full of struggle, hard work, and dreams for a better life. Although none of the women interviewed here are Zapatistas, they all share the dream of ethnic and gender equality, a vision that is part of the Zapatista dream of a dignified life for all Mexicans.

These particular women are distinctive, however, because they have chosen to lead lives that are usually forbidden to indigenous women. They are also unusual in that they have found success through sheer will and hard work outside the domestic arena. Xunka' sells hand-woven friendship bracelets in the park, attends high school and

---

[13]The PRD is the Party of Democratic Revolution led by Cuauhtémoc Cárdenas, and the PAN is the National Action Party whose candidate, Vicente Fox, won the 2000 presidential elections making him the first non-PRI president of Mexico in over 70 years.

takes photos that appear in books read by many people. Isabel is an actress and a playwright, who educates through popular theater about the reality of indigenous people. Lorenza is a weaver who learned about her rights as an indigenous woman by becoming part of an artisan cooperative.

## THREE MAYAN WOMEN
## IN SAN CRISTOBAL DE LAS CASAS

### 1. Camaristas—Photographers: Xunka'

*After failing to sell their Zapatista dolls and friendship brace-lets to the tourists in the park, the little Tzotzil girls try a new strat-egy. "Take my picture for a dollar," they tell the gringos. The tourists pull out their camera, fascinated by the opportunity to photograph these lovely girls with their colorful clothes, their cute braids, their beautiful smiles and their big brown eyes. The girls pose for the cam-era, half-serious, half-smiling. They retrieve their payment and run away. The tourists feel satisfied. They have added another picture to their collection of vacation photos.*

*These are the pictures that tourists take: pictures of "cute," "colorful," "folkloric" people that they can show to their friends back home. Then there are the pictures taken by professional pho-tographers—those that appear in glossy magazines, in* National Geo-graphic, *on postcards, and in framed portraits destined for living rooms. These are beautiful photos. They are works of art, but they don't tell us much about the real lives of the people, about their souls. Anthropologists also try to photograph the life of the indigenous. But often, they show people only as pieces of a museum. How different these photographs are from the ones we take of our family members and friends—photos taken with love.*

*But one group of Mayan women has set out to do exactly this. They photograph themselves and show their real world, their real lives, their loved ones, their animals and their work. These women are members of the Chiapas Photography Project and the Indigenous*

*Photography Archive.*[14] *Xunka' is one of these women. She is also a weaver and a street vendor who sells her bracelets in the central park of San Cristóbal. She is a high school student, and a member of* Sbeik Jchanvunetik *(Ways of Learning), a non-profit association.* Sbeik Jchanvunetik *is committed to the education of Mayan women. It provides them with literacy workshops, scholarships, and formal and informal education.* Sbeik Jchanvunetik *works with the San Cristóbal artisan street vendors, many of whom have been displaced from their home communities in Chamula.*

## Xunka"s Story [15]

My name is Xunka'. I was born in the hamlet of Jol Tzem'en, in the municipality of San Juan Chamula. I am 24 years old. I'm Tzotzil, and I'm a Presbyterian. I live in San Cristóbal de las Casas, in *Colonia Nueva Esperanza*. I work with this association called *Sbeik Jchanvunetik*. I'm an artisan, and I'm a high school student. I'm also a photographer.

I came to San Cristóbal with my family from Chamula when I was only four years old. I don't remember what it was like when I came. But I know we left our community in Chamula because of our religion. The people of San Juan Chamula don't like us because they're traditionalists and we're Presbyterian. The traditionalist Chamulas threw us out because we're Presbyterian—because we're Protestants. They say that since we're Protestants, we are no longer Indians and so we can't live in Chamula. But this isn't true. We are indigenous. We are Tzotzil. But we are also Presbyterian. We speak Tzotzil; we dress like Tzotzil Chamulas; we live like Tzotzil Chamulas; we *are*

---

[14]The Chiapas Photography Project was started by Carlota Duarte in 1992. It later became the Indigenous Photography Archive housed in the research institution, CIESAS-Sureste. The Archive preserves the work of over 200 indigenous men and women of various ethnic groups and promotes their work through publications and exhibitions. Among the books published by the Indigenous Photography Archives are *Creencias*, by Maruch Santiz Gómez (CIESAS,1998) and *Camaristas*, (CIESAS, 1999).

[15]Interview with Xunka' López Díaz in San Cristóbal de las Casas, May, 1997.

Tzotzil Chamulas. But we also go to a Presbyterian church and we believe in Jesus Christ our Savior. My parents told me that when they lived in San Juan Chamula they used to spend too much money buying alcohol for drinking. They also bought many candles whenever they were ill, and they went to the healer who charged them a lot of money, but they did not get cured. For these reasons, they never had money to buy food and they were always very poor. My father told me that one day when he was working in a plantation, he met a man who was evangelical and who told him about the Word of God. When my father returned from the plantation, he took my mother to the Evangelical Presbyterian Church in San Cristobal. And after that day, they continued going to the church, and they became believers. The *caciques* and authorities of my community started to organize the people to expel those who were Evangelical, like my parents. My mother was pregnant with her third baby when the "traditionalist" people came and took my father away from the house to the center of town, where they asked him to renounce his new religion. My father did not want to renounce his faith. So they told him to leave town or they would put him in jail. My parents fled that night and went to San Cristóbal, where they first stayed in the house of a man they knew. My mother was in a lot of pain the night they left, and my little brother was born when they got to San Cristóbal. My parents did not have clothes or blankets for the new baby. They suffered a lot when they came to San Cristóbal.

That's how we came to live in San Cristóbal. I don't remember much about this. I only remember my childhood here in San Cristóbal. I have eight brothers and sisters. Another brother died when he was little. When I was a child, I spoke only Tzotzil in my home, but when I went to elementary school, I learned to speak Spanish. We had good teachers and we had bad teachers. Some teachers told us not to worry, that we would learn little by little. Other teachers hit us with a stick if we couldn't learn Spanish.

When we moved to San Cristóbal, my father first worked as a helper on a construction crew, bringing water, running errands and carrying things for the workers. He didn't earn very much money, and he couldn't support his family with this work. We were only small children then, and we couldn't help him. Then my father went to work in the market, carrying produce on his back from the trucks to the stalls. But the produce was very heavy, and he hurt his back. Now he works as a carpenter. He's doing better now. The problem is that they don't always pay him on time. Sometimes it takes two or three months for people to pay what they owe him. We are very different from the *mestizos* of San Cristóbal. We have to work very, very hard to get what we need. We are indigenous expelled Chamulas. We can't speak Spanish properly. We are discriminated against and mistreated by the people in the city.

When I was a child, I started to sell woven bracelets and belts in the streets and in the park of San Cristóbal. I've been selling in the streets since I was very little. I could count and I could add and subtract, so I could sell. I could speak a little Spanish then, but I couldn't read or write very well. After I went to elementary school for a while, I met a woman named Catalina who invited me to join this association. The association is called *Sbeik J'chanvunetik*. It helps women, so they can learn to read and write. It helps us to continue with our education and attend junior high and high school. But a lot of the women who joined have become discouraged and have left. Only those of us who are willing to work hard and who want to learn are still here.

Right now we have six women and two men. Usually the Tzotzil men in San Cristóbal already know how to read and write. This isn't the case with the women because we have to go into the streets to sell our bracelets and our weavings from the time we are very little, to help our parents, because they work so hard. So, we drop out of school when we are little, and we never learn to read and write very well.

In the association we make handwoven bracelets and belts, and we sell them here in San Cristóbal. Our association gets money from concerned people and from the sale of our crafts, so that we can get scholarships to go to junior high and high school. Our adviser, Carlota Duarte, helps us a lot. We also work with the Indigenous Photography Archive as photographers. We have been invited to Mexico City and other cities, and to the United States and Europe to show our photographs in exibits. We travel with Carlota. We show our photos and sell our artisan work. We've published several books of photographs about our lives.[16] We also write little stories for our people to learn about hygiene and health. These are called photo-stories. They're like comic books with photographs, and they're for people to use in school—to learn with them. We didn't know how to take photographs before, but we learned. First we learned with disposable cameras. We didn't know how to use a camera, really. We were told to take pictures of whatever we wanted, so we did. We took pictures of our families, our animals, our neighborhoods and villages, our work tools, our *fiestas*—everything. That's how we became photographers. We call ourselves *camaristas*.

In January 1994, when the Zapatistas came, my parents told me I couldn't go out. After a while I went, but I didn't sell my crafts in the park that day because I was afraid. The policemen told us we shouldn't be there. When I finally saw the Zapatistas, I was surprised to see they were indigenous like me. My girlfriends weren't afraid. They even went to talk with the Zapatistas. We decided to make dolls that were like the Zapatistas, and we sold them in the park. This is how we started to make Zapatista dolls, because we were impressed by these people. The dolls sell very well with the tourists.

Right now I want to learn about everything. I'm learning how to type, how to use the computer, how to use the video and audio equipment, and how to develop the photographs. I want to learn everything. I think it's very important to learn to do everything to get ahead. Even if you're a woman, you must learn. Even if you are indigenous and poor, you must learn. Even if you are an expelled Tzotzil in San Cristóbal and people discriminate against you, you must learn.

---

[16]Xunka' López Díaz's book, *Mi hermanita Cristina* containing photographs and her testimonials will be published in January 2001 by CIESAS. It will be a trilingual edition in Tzotzil, Spanish and English.

## 2. *Teatristas*—Women of the Grassroots Theater: Isabel

*It was Saturday afternoon at the Centro Cultural El Carmen, a colonial church and convent in San Cristóbal that had been remodeled and turned into a cultural center with a library, a theater and classrooms for community education classes. This center also housed the Zapatista delegations when they came to town to meet with civil society organizations during the San Andrés peace negotiations between the EZLN and the Mexican Government in 1996.*

*We were sitting on folding chairs in an adapted outdoor auditorium in the front yard of El Carmen waiting for the show to start. The audience was made up of a variety of people from San Cristóbal: the so-called coletos; a bunch of young people dressed with colorful clothes and colorful hair; many Tzotzil children, including candy sellers, shoeshine boys, and street children; tourists of all kinds; and a large group of indigenous and mestizo working-class men and women, all sitting together. The show consisted of a marimba band, a local rock band, a Chiapas folk dance performed by a group of elementary school girls, and the main attraction—a play by a grassroots theater group called "The Strength of Mayan Women," or in Spanish,* Fortaleza de la Mujer Maya *(FOMMA). The theater group was made up entirely of indigenous women, residents of San Cristóbal.*

*Petrona and Isabel, the directors of FOMMA, had invited us to watch the play. It was a comedy portraying an urban working-class family, and it had an array of characters all played by the indigenous actresses of FOMMA. Two of the characters were an indigenous macho-but-loving husband and his docile and obedient wife. In addition, there were a bunch of street children of all ages, a nosy neighbor, and a helpful midwife who advised the mother on the value of birth control.*

*The play was received with laughter and screams of excitement from the very mixed audience. The high point of the comedy was a scene which was repeated over and over again. On stage there was a curtain, ostensibly leading to a bedroom. In the bedroom, a couple is making love, but the audience can only see two pairs of entangled naked feet emerging from the curtain. The giggles and murmurs of the man and woman are heard from behind a curtain. This scene is followed by that of the woman pregnant and the scene of the birth of a new baby. The sequence repeats until the couple has six children, and they finally decide to try family planning. (We wondered if it was not too late.)*

*This comedy had been successfully presented in parks, in schools, and in health centers of several Chiapas towns. As Isabel had told me, the play's objective was to educate people about the need for family planning.*

*Throughout the years, the women of FOMMA have dedicated themselves to educating indigenous people through grassroots theater on a variety of topics, particularly those that concern the lives and problems of the indigenous residents of San Cristóbal. A few days before I saw the play, I interviewed Isabel about her life and work.*

## Isabel's Story [17]

This is my life. I've been very lucky because I've met many kind and wonderful people who have helped me. It wasn't easy at first: I was born poor, I'm an indigenous woman, and I've had to work very hard. But here I am now, with Petrona, running this theater group of Mayan women. Other people helped us, and now we want to help by giving an opportunity to these women and children.

I was born in Aguacatenango. My first language is Tzeltal. I lived in that town as a child with my parents. When I was five years old there were problems with my father. He used to hit my mother all the time. My mother put up with this situation for many years, but there was a moment when she couldn't stand it anymore, and she decided to leave my father and go and live with my grandfather. She left us with our father.

My father used to work as a health promoter, and he had land and horses. After my mother left, my father sold everything we had—including our house—and we were left homeless. He took all the money, and he remarried. But he started doing badly, and he lost his

---

[17]Interview with Isabel of FOMMA in San Cristóbal de las Casas, 1997.

money. Then, he left his health promoter job and we all moved so he could go to work as a farm worker on a plantation near Tapachula. Life on the plantation was very hard. I became very ill with malaria when I was there. My father noticed how sick I was, and he took me to his mother's house. My grandmother went to tell my mother that I was very sick. My mother thought I was going to die. She took me to the public hospital in Tuxtla. When I recovered, I went to live with my mother and her father. My maternal grandfather was very good to me. He was a salesman, and he went to all the markets selling corn, squash, and wild fruit. I liked him very much, and I liked to go with him on his trips.

Later on, I went to live with my sister in the city of San Cristóbal. My sister was working as a maid with a lawyer and his wife. Then she got married and decided not to work anymore. I talked with her and told her that I could work for the family in her place. That's how I went to work as a maid. I was only nine years old. I cleaned the house and took care of the children, and I lived in their house. There was a school nearby, so I asked my employers if I could go there to study, and they said yes. That's how I learned to read and write. I was about 10 years old when I started elementary school. My employers helped me and encouraged me with my education. They paid the school tuition, and they even paid for private classes so that I could learn to type. I finished elementary school while I was working at their house. Then, I went on and finished junior high school. I was 18 years old when I finished. By then, I'd decided to stay in the city because I liked to study. I only went home to see my family during vacations.

I was very lucky that I worked with these people. Many indigenous women who come from the countryside don't have it so good. A lot of them are mistreated. They get paid very low wages, or they don't get paid at all and their only compensation is their room and board. There's a lot of racism and discrimination here in San Cristóbal, and the indigenous women are constantly humiliated. I learned this later on, when I worked in theater because I interviewed indigenous domestic workers to get material for our plays. But my life wasn't like that. I was extremely lucky to have had such wonderful employers. They were very nice to me. When I finished junior high school, I got married. I went to high school for one year but I had to quit when my husband had an accident. He was on a bus to Simojovel to visit his parents, and the bus crashed. That's how he died. When my husband died, I was two months pregnant. I quit school and went to work at an artisan store. I worked in the store, receiving the artisan products, paying the artisans and contracting people to make the products. When we ran out of something, I had to call the artisans to supply us.

While I was working there, I met a group of indigenous people who wrote and performed plays in Mayan languages. The group was called "Indigenous Culture," and the director was from Chamula. Others were from Zinacantán and Tenejapa. So, I started working with them. That was in 1983. After a while, I had problems with this group because I was the only woman. Even now I don't know why I was asked to leave. All they said was that they couldn't pay me anymore.

My son was one year old when I lost my job with the theater group. I went to work then with a committee for Guatemalan refugees. I left my baby with my mother and went to work in the refugee camps from 1984 to 1986.

I traveled to all the Guatemalan refugee camps in Las Margaritas and in Comitán, very close to the border. My work was to teach people about nutrition and health. I enjoyed working in the camps because I worked with indigenous people like me. They were Cakchikel and Mam Indians who had had fled Guatemala because of the war—because the Guatemalan army had destroyed their villages. I worked 10 days in each camp, and then I had to return for 10 days to San Cristóbal to give my reports. It was a great experience for me. I learned all about the conflict in Guatemala by talking with Guatemalan women and men about what they experienced. I learned about all the suffering they went through.[18]

After I finished my work with the Guatemalan refugees, the theater group invited me to work with them again. The group's name had been changed to "*Sna Tsibajom.*" I went to a meeting and all the men from the theater group were there. I told them that I wasn't going to let them do the same thing to me again, and that I'd come to do good work. They listened and we talked, so I stayed. This time I didn't work as a writer, but worked instead as a puppeteer. It was 1988 and we traveled to Mexico City, Veracruz and Puebla presenting our puppet plays. After working with the puppets I became the treasurer, because I am good with accounting. At that time we decided to start live plays with actors and to present traditional legends. In 1989 I acted for the first time in a play. We decided we needed more actresses. Petrona started to work with us, as well as a woman from Chenalho', another from Tenejapa and one from Zinacantán.

Whenever there was a meeting, however, the men didn't listen to the women. I was very aware of this, and I usually spoke up. I wouldn't allow the men to silence me. The women worked extra hard. We had to do lots of research and interviews in the communities. We interviewed indigenous women from Chiapas as well as Guatemalan refugee women that I had met before. That's how we wrote our plays, basing them on people's real lives and experiences. I had experience and knowledge of the women's problems. I chal-

---

[18]In the early 1980s, thousands of indigenous Mayans were murdered in Guatemala and hundreds of villages were completely destroyed by the Guatemalan security forces. During this time, tens of thousands of indigenous Guatemalans—civilian victims of the counterinsurgency war—crossed the Mexican border into Chiapas. The Diocese of San Cristóbal came to their rescue organizing small camps to receive them. The arrival of the Guatemalan refugees caused an upsurge in the activism of Chiapas civil society, and gave birth to may non-governmental organizations (NGOs). Many Mexicans began to travel to Chiapas in those years to help the Guatemalan refugees during their long stay in Mexican territory. The camps were eventually organized and sponsored by the United Nations High Commission of Refugees and legalized by the Mexican government. Still, much of the work, help and support came from NGOs and Mexican civil society. Refugees were not able to return in an organized fashion to Guatemala until the mid-1990s.

lenged the men on their *machismo*, and I challenged the women to try to discuss and teach about their own problems through these plays. Men argued that a woman's place was in her house, taking care of her children. I told them that women also want to get ahead, to study, to learn and to work, and that women want to solve our own problems.

In 1992, Petrona and I left the group. We decided to form our own theater group with indigenous women. We both had written several plays, so we knew how to put together a play. And we knew how to act, but we didn't have a place to perform. So we formed an indigenous women's street theater group, and we began performing in village plazas, in the streets, in schools and in auditoriums. We invited two other indigenous actresses to join us, and we started preparing our first play, *La mujer desesperada* (The Desperate Woman). This is a tragedy about domestic violence and violence in general. We performed this play in San Cristóbal on March 8, 1993, on International Women's Day.

There is a woman—an anthropologist—who helped us out a lot on this project. We didn't know how to write funding proposals, and she helped us. We were able to get some financial support, and in 1993 we were constituted as a legal non-profit association. We moved into a house on September 16, 1993. We didn't have any furniture, so we organized a party and invited a lot of people. We asked each person to bring a chair, or a table, or bookshelf or whatever. That's how we were able to furnish our house.

We named our organization FOMMA, which means *Fortaleza de la Mujer Maya* (Strength of Mayan Women). We started with a literacy project for women and children. There are many displaced women who come to live in San Cristóbal from Chamula and Zinacantán. They come for religious, political and economic reasons—because they are persecuted, or because they are very poor and come looking for work in the city. They sell little things in the streets and in the park, and they work as domestics or they wash clothes for other people. They learn a few words in Spanish, but they can't read or write. They suffer a lot because they remain poor, because they can't find good work and because people mistreat them.

Our literacy project was for these women.

We have also seen the children that live and work in the streets, and we've interviewed them. We ask them if they go to school. They say, "No, I sell candy in the streets." These are all indigenous children, mostly Tzotzil. Many of them live in the streets. Others live with their parents in shacks in *La Hormiga*. They have to go out to beg or to work in the streets in order to help their families. So we started inviting the children to come, too. Sometimes we have as many as 30 or 40 children. We also started other workshops for the women. In addition to literacy, we have workshops on popular theater, sewing and on how to make puppets with paper maché. In 1995 we also opened our childcare center.

We were renting a house, but it was too small for all our workshops, and the rent was high. We looked around for a house and figured out how much it would cost to buy it, and we got a loan from an agency. So we found this house. It was in terrible condition—very dark and damp, with rotten wood and moldy walls. We had to paint and change the windows and doors, because we were concerned that the children would get sick during the rainy season.

Now we are 11 women associates, plus all the women and children who come to the workshops. For the children we have the daycare center, an after school program, a Spanish literacy program, and a Tzotzil and Tzeltal literacy program—because the Mayan languages aren't taught in public schools. We have a library, a bakery, a sewing workshop to make clothes for the plays and for sale, and we have a small store. We make all our own puppets and masks for the plays. We have written about 20 plays now, plus many stories and poems. And we have several books published. We've traveled to the United States and Europe, and all over Mexico. We do adult plays, children's live theater and puppet theater.

Our plays are about the lives of the indigenous women and children who come to the city from the countryside and about the problems they encounter here—poverty, discrimination, abuse. . . They are about a lot of different topics: about alcoholism, domestic violence, racism and *machismo*; about living in the streets without education or work skills; about children who work in the market; about the abuse on the plantations or the poverty in the highlands; about the violence and repression against indigenous people; and about why they come to the city. We try to educate people about the need to defend their rights—about the need to unite and organize and to get an education for themselves and their children. We also deal with health, reproductive rights, women's rights, indigenous culture—even the environment. We try to do this with fun and humor. People laugh, but they understand the message. We also act out the traditions of our people—the legends and tales of the Tzeltal, Tzotzil, Chol and Tojolobal people. Many of our plays are in the Mayan languages because we perform in the villages.

We have a children's play about Mother Earth. The children perform it with their masks of the moon, the sun and the earth. They play the roles of bad people and good people, and the devil that tries to corrupt them. We have other plays about life on the plantations; or about what happens to the children when a family moves to San Cristóbal from the countryside; or what happens when we throw garbage in the ravines and our rivers become polluted. The children have fun even as they learn about humiliation and abuse, or about the *campesinos* working hard under the sun while the plantation owner is having a picnic. They also learn about their own responsibilities to their families, to society and to nature. We present plays like these so that the children think about these issues, and so that they understand the need for deep changes in our society. They start to think, "Is it really like this? Why is it like this? What is our future going to be? What can we do to change this situation so that we have a better future?"

So, that's what we do. We try to educate through our workshops and through theater. The women in our theater group and workshops have changed a lot. They know how to defend themselves now—in their jobs, in the marketplace and in their own homes. Their husbands have changed, too. There are a lot of men who come here now to help us. They want to learn about their own rights and responsibilities. And the people who watch our plays also learn. They learn that indigenous people have rights, and that we have a rich culture. They learn that indigenous Mayan women can do lots of things, and that we can do them well. There have been a lot of changes in Chiapas—and from Chiapas to the world— especially since 1994. We think that these changes are improving our lives, and we want to be part of them.

### 3. *Tejedoras*—Weavers: Lorenza

*On a sunny spring day, three indigenous women sit on the grassy plains in front of the Santo Domingo church in San Cristóbal de las Casas. They are oblivious to the sellers in the street market: Zinacanteca women selling beautiful table cloths embroidered with large flowers in bright pink and purple colors; expelled Chamulan women selling tightly woven vests of natural gray and black wool or finely hand sewn woolen stuffed animals and Zapatista dolls; and the local mestizo youth with long matted hair and '60s style "hippie" clothes selling fine handcrafted silver and amber jewelry. The women are also oblivious to the tourists walking from stall to stall trying to get the best bargain and to the Catholic worshipers leaving the 16th century church as they come from Mass.*

*They are Tzotzil women from the highlands, from the villages of Chenalho'—Magdalenas and San Andrés—I can tell by the designs of their blouses. They are laughing and talking in Tzotzil, thoroughly enjoying themselves as they engage in the timeless art of backstrap weaving. The women sit kneeling with their bottoms resting on top of their feet. Keeping their backs straight, they lean slightly backwards into a position that would appear totally uncomfortable for most Westerners. Each one of their bodies holds a loom, connected at one end to a belt around her waist and at the other end to a tree trunk. A rainbow of threads emerges out of their waists towards the trunk as they work the woof and warp up and down, back and forth. Their magic fingers move the threads, producing a beautiful brocade fabric of ancient designs.*

*I watch them for a long time. I never tire of watching indigenous women weave. I ask myself, "How do they remember the patterns of their great-grandmothers? How do they keep it all inside their heads?" Anthropologists have told me that each one of the designs in the fabrics has a symbolic meaning that carries the old se-*

*crets of the Mayans. Their blouses also tell what village a woman is from, whether she is young or old, single or married, and much about her creative personality. Backstrap weaving is an art that dates back to pre-Colombian times. It is, perhaps, the oldest surviving art of the Mayans. The designs in some of the weavings are the same as designs chiseled on the stones of the pyramids or painted on temple walls at the classical Mayan archeological sites, such as those of Palenque and Bonampak. Mayan women throughout Chiapas and Guatemala have kept this art alive. The weavers have not only kept the traditional designs from disappearing, but like modern-day Western fashion, they continuously evolve with more creative new designs, techniques, colors and materials.*

*In Chiapas, and particularly in the highlands, Mayan women continue to hand-produce their clothing and the clothing of their husbands and children. In the area of Chamula, women raise sheep, card wool, spin yarn and weave the material to make skirts for themselves and vests for their husbands. The cloth is as tight as felt and as water proof as raincoats. The women of Zinacantán embroider beautiful colorful flowers on their handwoven blouses, shawls and vests. The women of Magdalenas produce delicate wool and cotton blouses for ceremonies and weddings, and to dress up the icons of Mary Magdalene and the Virgin Mary in the church.*[19]

*Sadly, most Mayan women cannot afford to wear their finest weavings. It is common for the most beautiful and delicate woven textiles to be destined for museums or for the tourist trade where they can bring in much needed cash. In the highlands, women weave more simple blouses for themselves. In other parts of Chiapas, women may sew cotton or polyester blouses or go to the market to buy blouses—even T-shirts— to wear. In many areas of Chiapas, Indian women have forgotten how to weave all together.*

*Still, for many Mayan women of the highlands, weaving has become their only source of cash income. In San Cristóbal,*

---

[19]*The Living Maya* by Chip Morris is a fascinating and beautiful illustrated book on the modern Mayans. It is the best source of information on Chiapas textiles and the lives of the women who produce them.

*Zinacanteca women and expelled Chamulas sell in the markets or to the non-Indian owned artisan stores. In the last 20 years, Mayan women from the highlands have started organizing into artisan cooperatives to sell their handiwork collectively.*[20] *In the Chiapas highlands, the artisan cooperative movement has become—together with Christian base communities and the indigenous rights movement— one of the most important forms of organizing and awareness raising for Mayan women. Through these groups, they have advanced in their struggle for gender and ethnic identity, and in the knowledge of and defense of their own rights.*[21]

*One woman who learned about her rights through her collective artisan work is Lorenza. I met Lorenza at J'olom Mayatik, an artisan cooperative of indigenous women from the highlands.*[22] *On April 8, 1997, she spoke to the press and general public at the International Women's Day Rally in San Cristóbal de las Casas. She made public her testimony of how her human rights had been violated for her work in the cooperative and the indigenous civil rights movement. In the following months, I talked with her about her life, about her work as a weaver, and about the artisan cooperative.*

### Lorenza's Story[23]

My name is Lorenza and I'm a member of the *J'olom Mayatik* artisan organization. I'm 24 years old, and I'm single. I am an artisan. I weave hand-loomed wool fabrics, and I embroider blouses and other cotton textiles. I come from the municipality of Chenalho', from

---

[20]*Sna Jolovil, J'olom Mayatik* and *Mujeres por la Dignidad* are some of the women's artisan cooperatives in Chiapas.

[21]For more information, see articles by Christine Eber including, "Women Weavers in Highland Chiapas," *Crafts of the World Market: The Impact of Global Exchange on Middle American Artisans*, ed. June Nash (Albany: State University of New York Press, 1995), pp. 154-180 and "Las mujeres y el movimiento por la democracia en San Pedro Chenalho', *La Otra Palabra: Mujeres y violencia en Chiapas antes y después de Acteal*, CIESAS, Mexico, 1998, pp. 84-105.

[22]*J'olom Mayatik* is a member of the women's organization *Kinal Antzetik* that works with organized indigenous women in education, organization, training and technical assistance for weaving cooperatives.

[23]Interview with Lorenza of *J'olom Mayatik*, June 1997.

a hamlet called Pochib. Right now, I'm the coordinator of *J'olom Mayatik.*

There are six children in my family—three brothers and three sisters. When I was very little I didn't know how to behave, and my mother always gave me advice. She taught me how to work—how to pull the grains from the corncobs, feed the chickens, grind the corn in the *nixtamal,* and how to make *tortillas.*[24] Later on, my mother taught me how to make our clothes, because we always make our own clothes. We make everything. We sew and embroider our blouses, and we weave our skirts and our belts. We also make the men's clothes. In other towns, the women also weave their blouses called *huipiles.*

My mother also took me to the countryside with her and taught me how to take care of the sheep. We always carried our handiwork with us, and while we were in the mountains watching the sheep, we sat down to embroider or weave. Weaving was the last thing I learned to do, because weaving is very hard.

When we make our skirts, first we weave a large piece of wool fabric on what's called a backstrap loom. Then we wash it with hot boiling water to shrink it, and we dye it black with a natural dye while we boil it. I learned, little by little, to weave and wash and dye the wool for our skirts. We also weave our belts, which are made of cotton in many colors. We weave everything on backstrap looms.

I will tell you how this cooperative was formed. My mother and another woman started a cooperative in the village of Pochib in 1984. At that time, there were about 10 women in Pochib who liked to weave and who were interested in selling their products. A man named Pellicer, who was a lawyer from Chenalho', came to talk with them, and he told them that he wanted to buy their textiles. So, the women got their textiles together, and took them to him. Then they formed an organization and began to work together. It wasn't *J'olom Mayatik* yet. It was called *Sna Jolobil.*

---

[24]*Tortillas* are thin, round cakes made of cornmeal that are the staple food, or bread, of the indigenous people. *Nixtamal* is stone-ground cornmeal made into a dough. It is the base for *tortillas, tamales* and drinks such as *pozol* and *atol.*

When I was little, I worked with my mother in this first cooperative. There were about four communities in Chenalho' where the women organized to sell their handwoven and embroidered textiles. In the past, women only worked picking coffee. But then we decided that we could do artisan work, and we joined together in the village of Pochib to do so. With time, more and more women joined the group. They learned that they could sell their artisan work. We took our products to San Cristóbal to sell, and eventually we found a house there where we could sell them. Later, we sold our textiles at the National Indigenous Institute.

At first we didn't get enough money for all our work. Our textiles were sold at for really low prices. We had to walk all the way to San Cristóbal from our village, and it was a long way! At that time the road wasn't paved, and our feet ached from all that walking. Now, it has changed a lot! Now there's a paved road to my village, and we can travel by bus. The cooperative even pays our bus fare. Also, now we get more money for our textiles. We get a good price. My mother and the other women now participate fully in the life of the organization. This is good because in the past, women only did their work at home, and they didn't get involved in anything else.

We worked with the *Sna Jolobil* cooperative until 1994. But in 1995 we separated and formed another cooperative. Later on, some of us separated again from the second cooperative, and that's when we formed *J'olom Mayatik*. It was because we wanted to know more about our rights that we separated.

After 1994, we learned we had rights as indigenous women. Unfortunately, in our communities of *Los Altos,* men drink too much alcohol and they beat their wives. We learned that there are laws that protect women—laws we can use to defend ourselves. When we first heard about these laws, we wanted to learn more about them. Some of the women in the organization said, "We want to learn our rights. We want to learn all those things we don't know." Other women didn't want to learn about these things. So, that's when we divided. A few of us who wanted to know more left to start *J'olom Mayatik*. The other women only wanted to sell their artisan work. They only wanted to weave and embroider. But we wanted to take a new road.

We wanted to open our eyes.

According to these laws, women should be able to express our opinions. But the men in our communities don't respect our words. They don't let us talk. What we see in our communities is that women don't participate in the meetings. Only men participate, and they elect other men. So the women said we wanted to participate in the meetings, too. In my village, some men are now starting to accept our participation. But many people still don't understand or accept this.

In 1994 when I was working at the other cooperative, we started to receive threats. Those who threatened us knew what we were doing. They knew that we were taking a different road. Members of the security police came to the store asking questions. They asked for all of our names and asked us where we were from. Later on, other men came. I think they were military men, but they were dressed as civilians. That was in 1994 and 1995. Our adviser also received threats. We were all receiving threats that year. It was because we wanted to speak up—to have our say.

I'd never spoken up before. When I lived in my village, I couldn't even speak Spanish. I didn't know I had any rights. I didn't know that I could express my own opinions. Then, when I came to live in San Cristóbal—well, more or less—I started to speak my own mind.

There was a robbery at the store, too. Somebody broke in to steal sewing machines, typewriters, telephones—that type of stuff. It was really strange because around the time the robbers broke into the store, we'd been getting phone calls. We were told that if we didn't stop working there, they were going to kill us. Men and women called. I don't know who they were. This happened in 1995. That's when we got really scared and we left the second group.

When we started *J'olom Mayatik*, I used to do all my sewing and weaving in my house. We used to bring our textiles to San Cristóbal every three or four months. In San Cristóbal we would get information on what we needed to do. That's how we worked. I worked together with several women in my house, at my village. Then, the women who used to work in the store in San Cristóbal left the job. There was a general assembly at my organization with all the representatives from all the communities, and I was asked to work at the store. That's when I was elected coordinator.

Let me tell you what happened to me and one of my co-workers the other day. We'd been at the store to check on a literacy workshop our group started. We left around 7:30 at night, and we were walking in the street when a couple of guys came over. They tried to grab us, but we moved away from them. Then, they tried to grab us again and take our bags. We didn't know these men, except we knew they were Tzotzil.

This happened a second time. We left the store early one day, and we saw that there was a car parked outside the store with the same guys in it. As we walked away, the men got out of the car and started to run after us. We started to run too. They caught up with us at the next block. They grabbed us, and one of them tried to rip my blouse open. The other guy grabbed my friend and wouldn't let go. They were trying to rape us. They were trying to push us into the car, but we wouldn't let them. We fought. They told us that we were whores, and that we were Zapatistas. I picked up a stone and threw it at them. Finally, we were able to get away from them, and we ran away. We went to report this to the police.

We always participate in the marches, in the meetings and the rallies. These men have seen us in marches, and that's why they call us whores. These men don't want changes. They don't want equality. They think that men are bigger and more important than women. But, they don't even like themselves, because they also think that *ladinos*[25] are better and more important than we Indians. These men want to be like the *ladinos*, like the *kashlanes*.[26] They want to be macho and mistreat women. They don't want equality.

---

[25]*Ladinos*—Spanish term used exclusively in southern Mexico and Guatemala to designate people of mixed Indian and Spanish descent (just as the term *mestizos* is used throughout Mexico and much of the rest of Latin America). *Ladino* also designates the Indian that moves to the city, wears western clothes, stops speaking the Indian language and acts like non-Indian urban people.

[26]*Kashlanes*—Mayan word from the highlands of Chiapas that means white person. It is used by Mayan people to designate all those persons who are not Indian—foreigners and Mexicans alike.

Before 1994, women never participated. We didn't know about women's rights or about people's rights. After 1994—after the Zapatista uprising—both women and men started to organize. We went to the meetings and we came back with information. We all started talking with our families about what we'd learned. We began to think, "What should we do to stop the suffering? What should we do to stop the poverty?" We talked about organizing. We talked about learning our rights—people's rights, women's rights. We talked about what a problem it is for everyone when men drink. When men drink, there's not a cent left for the family. As women, we want men to help us with the chores. We can also work in the field. We always did, and we always do. So, we want equality between men and women. We also want equality between indigenous people and *ladinos*. We don't want to be discriminated against just because we speak another language besides Spanish, because we dress differently than the *coleto* people here or because our skin is darker. We won't allow this discrimination. If we all know our rights, then we can advance as people.

✳

# THREE

## Zapatista Civilians
## Organizing in the Midst of War

# THE ZAPATISTA MOVEMENT AND THE STRUGGLE FOR AUTONOMY

When the Zapatista uprising occurred in 1994, it was at a time when many middle-class Mexicans believed that Mexico was entering the First World through the North American Free Trade Agreement (NAFTA). The image being projected nationally, as well as internationally, was one of a pluralistic and democratic, "modern" Mexico, a country where strong opposition political parties existed for the first time in its history. But the Zapatista uprising and the subsequent indigenous rights movement challenged that image. Suddenly on January 1, 1994, Mexicans were forced to recognize that our country was not yet a democracy and that it is not part of the First World. We were no longer able to ignore the existence of Chiapas, the "deep south" of Mexico where inequality, extreme poverty and racism still exist. Beyond even that, Mexicans realized that the marginalization that exists in Chiapas exists throughout Mexico, and that we are still very far away from being a country in which all citizens enjoy equality of rights and benefits.

In the last decade of the 20th century, in the post-Cold War era of globalization and neoliberalism, a group of impoverished Mayan Indians in the mountains and rainforests of southeastern Mexico awoke the world with the cry of "Ya Basta!" "Enough is enough!"

## *The Zapatista Uprising*

On January 1, 1994—the same day that NAFTA went into effect for Canada, the United States and Mexico—a poorly armed Zapatista National Liberation Army (EZLN) rose up against the Mexican Army. Quietly, quickly, they took over four cities in the state of Chiapas (Ocosingo, Altamirano, Las Margaritas and San Cristóbal de las Casas). Not a shot was fired.

In San Cristóbal de las Casas, local inhabitants and tourists coming home from parties or on their way to the early New Year's Day Mass were surprised to see that the city had been taken over by a group of indigenous men and women. Many of the rebels were barefoot. They wore cheap Army uniforms. They covered their faces with ski-masks or bandannas, and they carried sticks or hunting rifles. Only a few insurgents—those that were known as *comandantes*, or commanders—carried weapons appropriate for war.

This was not a violent takeover by any means. Curious people even approached the indigenous guerrillas with questions. Soon, a Spanish-speaking man wearing a ski-mask emerged as a spokesperson. He was Subcomandante Marcos, military leader of the EZLN. From the municipal building of San Cristóbal de las Casas, Marcos read the Declaration of the Lacandón Rainforest, in which the Zapatistas declared war on the Mexican State and stated their 12 demands: freedom, democracy, justice, peace, land, education, health, housing, food, development, cultural rights and women's rights. All of these were summarized in the Zapatista slogan: *Justicia, Democracia y Libertad* (Justice, Democracy and Freedom).

By stating these demands, the EZLN was letting the world know that the most basic human rights still are not accessible to a majority of indigenous people in the impoverished rural areas of Mexico. At the end of the 20th century, an army of peasants felt that they had to rise up in arms against the state to demand rights as basic as health and education for their people. They also were demanding the right to preserve their cultural traditions, to remain on their lands, to gain access to enough land to survive and to determine their own path to development. In short, they were saying "no" to the dominant economic system and demanding a say in their own future.

In a matter of minutes, the news of the Zapatista rebellion spread throughout the world as international media received faxes sent from the humble offices of a local San Cristóbal newspaper, *El Tiempo.*[1] Before the Mexican government could respond, residents of the United States, Canada, Europe and Latin America were reading in their morning newspaper about the barefoot Indian army that called itself the EZLN. They were reading about the mysterious Subcomandante Marcos, about the centuries of oppression suffered by the indigenous peoples of America, and about the Zapatistas' 12 demands.

---

[1]As related to the author in an interview with Conchita Villafuerte, editor of *El Tiempo.*

# CHIAPAS AUTONOMOUS MUNICIPALITIES

● Aguascalientes
(cultural centers)

Source: the non-governmental
organization, *Enlace Civil*

Automous Municipalities
1. Libertad de los Pueblos Mayas
2. San Pedro de Michoacán
3. Tierra y Libertad
4. 17 de Noviembre
5. Miguel Hidalgo y Costilla
6. Ernesto Ché Guevara
7. Primero de Enero
8. Cabañas
9. Maya
10. Francisco Gómez
11. Ricardo Flórez Magón
12. San Manuel
13. San Salvador
14. Huitiupán
15. Simojovel
16. Sabanilla
17. Vicente Guerrero
18. Trabajo
19. Francisco Villa
20. Independencia
21. Benito Juárez
22. La Paz
23. José María Morelos y Pavón
24. San Andrés Sacamch'en de los
    Pobres
25. San Juan de la Libertad, El Bosque
26. San Pedro Chenalhó
27. Santa Catarina
28. Bochil
29. Zinacantán
30. Magdalenas de la Paz
31. San Juan Kankuj
32. Iztapa
33. Jitotol
34. Nicolás Ruíz

### The Zapatista Movement

The Zapatistas named themselves after Emiliano Zapata, a hero of the 1910 Mexican Revolution. With the cry of "Land and Freedom," Zapata rallied an army of indigenous peasants in the southern state of Morelos. His struggle changed history by leading to a far-reaching agrarian reform guaranteed by Article 27 of the Mexican Constitution. Article 27 established the *ejido*, a system for distributing land communally to landless peasants. Although not all *campesinos* received land, Article 27 provided the hope that someday they would.

In 1992, Article 27 was "reformed" under President Carlos Salinas de Gortari in order to comply with US requisites for Mexico's entry into NAFTA. The new modifications effectively turned *ejido* land into private property, allowing it to be sold to the highest bidder. The dreams that poor people had of someday owning land had ended. As subsistence farmers who lived from the fruit of their land, the Zapatistas cited the changes in Article 27 as one of the causes for their uprising.

The modern day Zapatista movement of Chiapas began in the Lacandón rainforest in 1983. It started as a small group of revolutionaries who were members of an urban guerrilla organization called the National Liberation Forces—young urban activists who had opted for armed struggle in the years following the 1968 massacre of students in Tlatelolco plaza. After years of organizing, the Zapatistas grew from this core group to a social movement made up of thousands of indigenous Tzotzil, Tzeltal, Tojolabal and Chol people throughout northern and eastern Chiapas, *Las Cañadas*, the rainforest, and the highlands.

With their 1994 uprising, the Zapatistas emerged as a new and different type of Latin American revolutionary movement. Much of their history had been in grassroots organizing in the Lacandón rainforest among Mayan and *mestizo* peasants who observe ancient Indian traditions of community work and communal decision making by consensus. These indigenous traditions shaped the Zapatista movement.

Today's Zapatistas are spiritual Mayan people, many of whom have been members of Christian base communities. For this reason, and in spite of being called an "army" (although close to 90 percent of the Zapatistas are civilians), Zapatistas are peace-loving people, with high moral standards and a deep commitment to social justice. More than an army, the Zapatista movement is a social movement of indigenous people. It is a civil rights movement that struggles for equality among all people. It is an indigenous rights movement of native peoples who want to govern their territories and manage their own resources. It also has been called a cultural revolution and a *campesino* justice movement.

The Zapatista movement also strives to be truly democratic. Unlike the Marxist-Leninist revolutions and Latin American guerrillas of the 1950s to 1980s, the Zapatistas are not interested in taking power. They are not interested in taking over the government of Mexico. Rather, they are interested in working at the grassroots level together with Mexican society, to build democracy from the bottom up. The Zapatista slogan of "*mandar obedeciendo,*" loosely translated as "to lead by following" is based on the Indian tradition of community service. Authorities are designated by the people, and they are servants of their people. This is the way that Zapatistas understand democracy.

The inclusion of women in positions of leadership and the incorporation of women's rights as one of the goals of the revolution is another great difference between the EZLN and traditional Marxist Latin American guerrillas. The Zapatista Army has included women at all levels of its military and political posts from the beginning. About half of the EZLN *comandantes* are women, and in the region of Morelia, in *Las Cañadas*, women hold a majority of leadership positions. Despite the fact that the Mexican indigenous culture has been a male-dominated culture since colonial times, participation and decision-making by women is encouraged in areas of Chiapas populated by Zapatista civilians. Women participate in assemblies and organizations. They are encouraged to speak of and promote their rights, and they have learned to speak up and defend themselves.

In March 1993, eight months before their January 1 uprising, the EZLN drafted a series of laws establishing the rights of indigenous women. Although the Revolutionary Women's Laws were drawn from consultations with many women over a period of several months, the idea that women had rights was a novel concept to many people in the highlands. By studying the Zapatista laws, women learned that they could choose who to marry and how many children to have. They learned that they had the right to study and to participate in the political and social life of the community, that they could organize outside of the home, and that these laws protected them from physical abuse.[2]

### The Growth of the Movement and the Call for Negotiations: 1994 to 1997

The armed conflict in Chiapas lasted only 12 days. The EZLN withdrew almost immediately from the cities it had taken over, and the Mexican Army entered with full force, occupying indigenous communities in *Las Cañadas* and the rainforest. Civilians living in the mountainous areas surrounding San Cristóbal fled to safer places as the Army sent bullets flying into their settlements. In Ocosingo, the EZLN was still in town when the Mexican Army arrived. In the ensuing battle, there were casualties on both sides as well as among civilians. During the days of this first Army offensive, human rights organizations documented an alarming number of human rights violations by the Mexican Army.[3]

But soon, Mexican citizens—with international support—demanded an end to the military violence and called for dialogue between the EZLN and the Mexican federal government. The two sides declared a ceasefire, and the first stage of peace negotiations started in February 1994 in the Cathedral of San Cristóbal de las Casas. Subcomandante Marcos and other Zapatista representatives met with a spokesperson of the Mexican federal government, and Bishop Samuel Ruíz was the mediator. In the spring, however, negotiations

---

[2]See the Zapatista *Revolutionary Women's Laws* on p. 225.

[3]*Chiapas, El Alzamiento* (La Jornada Ediciones, Mexico D.F., 1994) pp. 95-143.

were interrupted after the assassination of PRI presidential candidate, Donaldo Colosio, apparently by members of his own party. Civilian Zapatista communities feared that the political chaos brought on by this crime would have repercussions in Chiapas, so the EZLN did not return to the negotiating table.

In August 1994, the EZLN invited Mexican civil society groups to a make-shift "convention center" in the Lacandón rainforest village of Guadalupe Tepeyac to discuss national problems and propose ways to work towards peace, democracy, justice and freedom. The Zapatistas called this place an *aguascalientes* to evoke the memory of the city in central Mexico called Aguascalientes, where the armies of Emiliano Zapata and Francisco Villa had met with the representatives of the revolutionary government to draft the Federal Constitution in 1917.[4]

Thousands of people came from all over Mexico to the Chiapan rainforest in August 1994. It was the beginning of a civil society movement to support the Zapatista vision for a democratic transformation of Mexico and for a peaceful solution to the war. The term "civil society" has been used quite extensively in Mexico. It refers to the entirety of organized citizens' groups including grassroots organizations, unions, professional guilds, social groups and members of non-profit organizations. The term is an important one for countries like Mexico where the major decisions of the country have been made historically by a few elite actors in business, military and government without much input from its citizens or "civil society."

In February 1995, the Mexican government violated the declared ceasefire and staged a military offensive against the EZLN. Civilian Zapatista communities were invaded both in the rainforest and in

---

[4]An *aguascalientes* is a Zapatista cultural center, a campus that is used for political, cultural and educational meetings. These centers are simple constructions made from natural materials. They are built in order to house, feed, entertain and educate people of civil society—indigenous people, Mexicans or international friends. There are five *aguascalientes* in Chiapas: 1) La Realidad, a Tojolobal center in the Lacandón rainforest; 2) Oventik in the Tzotzil region of the highlands; 3) Morelia, in the Tzeltal region of *Las Cañadas*; 4) La Garrucha, in the multi-ethnic Lacandón *Cañadas* and rainforest; and 5) Roberto Barrios, in the northern region of Chiapas.

*Las Cañadas,* and arrest warrants were issued for Zapatista leaders. The Army dismantled and destroyed the *aguascalientes* cultural center in Guadalupe Tepeyac, and the people of Guadalupe fled deeper into the Lacandón forest where they established a new village. Today, the original Guadalupe Tepeyac is like a ghost town. Its houses are abandoned and overgrown weeds cover what at one time were its streets. In the place of the tropical village, there is now a military encampment with a large, but empty, government hospital. Other villages were also invaded, but townspeople eventually returned when the Mexican Army moved out.

In response to the destruction of their cultural center, the EZLN built five new *aguascalientes*: in the village of La Realidad in the Lacandón rainforest; in La Garrucha, also in the Lacandón rainforest; in Oventik in the highlands; Morelia in *Las Cañadas,* and Roberto Barrios in northern Chiapas. These five cultural centers are the capitals of the five regions where the Zapatista's have a presence in the northeastern portion of Chiapas.

Peace talks between the EZLN and the Mexican government began again in early 1996 after much pressure from Mexican civil society groups. A law protecting the Zapatistas from arrest and from Army invasions into their civilian communities also helped to pave the way for the talks that were held in the highland village of San Andrés Larrainzar (renamed San Andrés Sacamch'en de los Pobres by the Zapatistas). Four topics were to be discussed in the negotiations: Indigenous Rights and Culture, Democracy and Justice, Land and Agrarian Rights, and Indigenous Women's Rights.

One of the four topics —that of Indigenous Rights and Culture—was successfully discussed in San Andrés, and in February 1996, accords that became known as the San Andrés Accords were signed on this issue. However, despite the fact that a bill was drafted by COCOPA in November 1996 to incorporate these accords into specific legislation, the Mexican government refused to take the final step of signing it into law.[5] Negotiations were not officially broken off, but the two parties never sat together at the negotiating table again. From that moment on, the Mexican government's policy towards Chiapas became a combination of "talk about peace" (not peace talks) and a low intensity war that included a military belt of intimidation and harassment around the civilian Zapatista communities. It also came to include the encouragement, formation and training of paramilitary groups to attack Zapatistas and their sympathizers.

In the meantime, the Zapatista movement grew in membership and strength. According to the EZLN, there are 1,111 villages in 34 municipalities that are populated with "Zapatista civilians" or "Zapatista bases of support." These communities and municipalities call themselves "communities in resistance" or "autonomous communities."[6]

Even though the San Andrés Accords on Indigenous Rights and Culture were never signed into national law, the Zapatistas decided to apply the concepts of the accords in their own communities. An important part of this has been the declaration of autonomous communities. Indian autonomy is not a completely new concept in Mexico, since previous "practices and customs" legislation also allowed for some measure of autonomy. Based on the San Andrés accords, however, the Zapatistas have taken the concept of autonomy a step farther. Zapatista autonomous communities work independently of federal and state government, have their own economic, judicial and political systems, elect their authorities by consensus in open assemblies, apply the traditional Mayan system of community service and collective work, and develop at their own rhythm, with special atten-

---

[5]The Commission of Concord and Peace (COCOPA), made up of congressional and senatorial representatives from all political parties, is the organization whose mandate is to make sure the ceasefire is not broken, that negotiations continue and that signed accords are honored. In November 1996, COCOPA drafted the proposal for the Accords on Indigenous Rights and Culture to be signed into legislation. The Mexican government, however, refused to take the final step to sign them.

[6]See map and list of autonomous communities on p. 101.

tion to community needs.[7] It is important to note, however, that the Zapatistas are not a separatist movement. They want to exercise autonomy while remaining part of Mexico.

In this chapter, life in these so-called "autonomous communities" or "communities in resistance" is described through the voices of Zapatista civilians in the towns of Morelia in *Las Cañadas,* Oventik in the highlands, and San José del Río and La Realidad in the rainforest.

## THE LIVES OF ZAPATISTA CIVILIANS

### 1. Morelia: Voices from Las Cañadas

"This is what we think: If we organize, we will get what we need. If not, who will give it to us? If we don't search, we won't find it. If we don't struggle, it will not be there for us."

—Woman from Morelia

*The eastern part of the state of Chiapas is crisscrossed by a system of deep canyons, ravines and rivers that divide mountain ranges. This geographic area is called* Las Cañadas, *a Spanish word that loosely translates as "the canyons."* Las Cañadas *can be quite deep and spectacular with peaks shooting up on both sides, or they can be just shallow creekbeds and ravines. As a region,* Las Cañadas *is like a system of deep underground highways that divide the land. They are lush, green, deep roads and rivers that connect the pine forest in the highlands to the tropical lowlands rich with fruit trees and cattle-grazing lands of northern Chiapas to the Lacandón*

---

[7]The existing "Practices and Customs" legislation states that indigenous ethnic groups have the right to govern their communities in their own traditional way (usually assembly meetings with decision making by consensus, but different groups have different traditions). The COCOPA legislation proposal from the San Andrés Accords on Indigenous Rights and Culture adds more precise language for constitutional changes that would support indigenous autonomy. For more information on autonomous communities, see *SIPAZ Bulletin,* August 1998.

*rainforest on the Guatemalan border.*

*The Mayan Tzeltal town of Morelia is in the official municipality of Altamirano and, at the same time, the seat of an autonomous municipality called* Diecisiete de Noviembre, *or November Seventeeth. It is located in the central valley of Chiapas, in the region of* Las Cañadas. *It is also home to one of the Zapatista* aguascalientes, *or cultural centers.*

*I arrived for the first time to this village one afternoon, having traveled in three public vehicles to get there. I got off the bus with my backpack and walked down the perfectly aligned dirt roads, followed by giggly children and barking dogs. I had a letter from a non-governmental organization with an introduction and a request for a permission to do interviews. The children guided me to a house that, like most of the others, was just a small wood-frame hut. The "front porch" contained just a bench to sit on in front of the door and a straw mat on the dirt floor filled with coffee beans drying in the sun. This was the house of the "peace-campers."[8] I was welcomed by a young Mexican woman who shared her beans and rice with me and then introduced me to the town's representatives. I returned several times over the next two months to talk with townspeople and interview them.*

*In the following testimonies, several men and women of Morelia joined together to talk to me about the history of the town, its traditions, its effort to function autonomously, and the effects of the war on the community. They also express their feelings, their dreams and their hopes for the future.*

---

[8]Peace Campers—After the February 1995 military offensive into Zapatista territory, when indigenous civilians had to flee into the mountains, Mexican human rights groups organized to establish "peace camps." These camps were set up in several towns—particularly those of Zapatista influence—to protect civilians there from harassment. "Peace campers" are international and Mexican activists who stay at the peace camps for a period of weeks or months in order to be witnesses and to denounce abuses should they occur.

## a. Life in Morelia[9]

### How We Live

A MAN SPEAKS: The town of Morelia is about 75 years old. People came here from the towns of Altamirano and Chanal. They came from the neighboring plantations and from the mountains. The first people here were landless peasants who came to work as agricultural workers because this town was a plantation, what we call a *finca*. This land had an owner and the people here worked as peasants—*campesinos*. It was a tough life to work here. The *campesinos* worked very hard and they were paid almost nothing. Even a few years ago, we still only earned five pesos a day for work at the plantations. I don't know if the workers rebelled and took the land or if little by little they saved money and bought it. I don't know how they did it, but eventually the workers became the owners of this land. This town became an *ejido* and the land belonged to everybody communally. It was called Ejido Morelia and it became part of the Municipality of Altamirano. Today, Morelia is part of an autonomous municipality called *Diecisiete de Noviembre* (November Seventeenth).

In this town we are all Tzeltal. We all speak Tzeltal. Some people also speak Spanish. Most people here are Catholic. We don't drink here. No, I used to drink. I used to get very drunk, but I was told, "If you want to be part of the struggle, you cannot drink, because if you drink you can't help the struggle." When I'm drunk, I talk too much. I say everything. In the struggle you can't talk too much because it's dangerous. Also, if you are drunk you can't work, and we need workers. My wife is happy now because I work hard.

There was a priest who came here and taught people how to work. Before he came, people were mean to each other, but this priest wanted us to work together. This priest helped to build the town, the streets, the church, everything. He's not here anymore, though. He left a long time ago.

---

[9]Interviews conducted in Morelia, Altamirano (or Diecisiete de Noviembre) in December 1996 and January 1997.

Now we don't have a priest here. Every six months a priest comes and we have weddings and baptisms. We only have a deacon now—somebody from here. We used to have very good priests. They could explain the Word of God very well. But they left. Later on Father Vicente came. He was a very good priest, but he left too.

I'll tell you about our traditions here. I'll tell you about how the young people get married. This tradition has changed a little with the modern times, but we still maintain some of the old ritual. Three months before the wedding is the *pedida*, which is when the young man's parents go to ask for the hand of the young woman. They take bread, sodas, and two kilos of meat for the girl's parents. The young man doesn't go to the *pedida*. People here might tell you that the young man and young woman have never met before, and that they have never talked to each other, but it is seldom like this. That's the way it was in the past, not now. These days the young people talk with one another before the *pedida*. They know one another well. They maybe have already decided on their own to get married. They know each other well because they work together in the collective projects.

First, the boy's parents talk with the girl's parents. When they are at her house talking, they call the girl and tell her that their son wants to marry her. She has a week to decide whether she wants to get married. A week later the young man's parents return with him, to see what the young woman has decided. After this, if she accepts, the young man can visit her at her home once a week, until the wedding.

Our son who lives in Comunidad Siete de Enero is getting married next month. For his wedding we'll kill a calf. People here don't have much money. Sometimes people have nothing to offer at a wedding. Most young men wait to marry until they have their own home. Once married, they live apart from their parents. If they do end up living with their parents after they get married, they live with the family of the groom. After the February 1995 offensive, we had to flee to the mountains and to the jungle. Some of the young people decided to stay and settle in the mountains. They formed new communities there. One of the new communities is called Siete de Enero.

Most newly-weds from here live in Siete de Enero. It's a town of young people: of single men, of young couples and young families.

We only marry one spouse, not more. If a man wants to take another wife, he goes to jail because it's against the law. Women marry whoever they please. They marry men from here or from another town. If a woman marries a man from another town, she goes with him to the other town. Some women with children don't have a husband. They meet a man from another town, he goes away and the young woman lives here without a husband.

### How We Organized

A WOMAN SPEAKS: I was born here in Morelia. I am married, and I have eight children. They are all grown up. My oldest son is 25 years old. He is married and lives in a neighboring community called Siete de Enero. My second son is 20 years old. He's getting married next month. There are weddings in Morelia every six months. All the young people who want to get married, do it then.

We don't have a priest here. What we have is a *tunel*, which means "the servant" in Tzeltal. The *tunel* is like a priest. He's the one who performs weddings and baptisms. Most of us are Catholic here, and we Catholics work with the church. There are catechists and Delegates of the Word, too. Every Sunday we meet for Service. Every Sunday we read from the Bible and then we break into groups to talk. We ask one another what the Bible said, what the Word of God is and what it teaches us. We all go to talk about this in six groups: two men's groups, two women's groups, one group for the girls, and one for the boys. We have to write what we heard in the Bible readings. The secretary goes by every group to see what they understood.

We see that everything that happens here in Morelia is also in the Bible. We read in the Bible about the suffering of Jesus, about the Last Supper and the 12 Apostles. We read that they ate together and worked together, and that only one of them left. It says in the Bible that you need to look for your own answers. It tells you what you need to know and how to find solutions to your problems. It says that

Jesus died for the *campesinos*, not for the rich. So, that's how we started to organize.

Many years ago a priest came. I think it was in 1975. This priest asked us, "Why are the *campesinos* suffering?" He told us, "Why don't we work together like it says in the Bible? Because Jesus said we all have loaves and we all have fishes, and we all need to share what we have. Everything should be for everybody. Everything should be for all the *campesinos*." Well, that's the way we started. Some people didn't like the priest. They said, "How does he know this?" They didn't understand because they didn't listen. We didn't want to believe anything in those days. The men were only interested in drinking. People didn't listen when they went to church, and the words of the priest were lost. When he left we forgot his words, and we didn't do what he told us to do. The wind took his words away, and we stayed the same as before. But there were some catechists who understood the Word of God. With them, we began to remember, and we began to analyze the words that the priest left for us.

Then we organized. The women said, "Why don't we all do like Jesus? Why don't we work together?" That's how we started to organize. It was the same in the other communities throughout *Las Cañadas*.

### How Does Autonomy Work?

MEN AND WOMEN SPEAK: Our organization as autonomous communities grew because there are women and men who think in a very clear manner. If a person understands clearly, she speaks clearly. We organized from community to community throughout *Las Cañadas*. By 1991 we were many women and many men, and we were very well organized. It wasn't like this before. At the beginning, women didn't want to participate, and men didn't allow them to participate. Later on, everybody understood that it was important for us all to work.

We have two kinds of organizations: one is for working on production projects, and another is for organizing politically as an autonomous structure. The two organizations are linked by the same goal. They work together so that we can have autonomy, or self- government.

This is the history of our economic organization: We used to be members of *ARIC-Union de Uniones.*[10] We were members of ARIC in Ocosingo, but that was too far away. We had a lot of problems getting there. And life is different in Ocosingo. They have other needs. It didn't work for us. So we left *ARIC,* and we started *Tzomán,* to work on our own projects. In the Tojolobal language, *Tzomán* means "unite to work together." Now we work independently of these organizations. We work on our own on the whole project of autonomy. Our economic organization is for our work—for our projects. First we identify the needs of the community, then we propose the projects. Then we look for the money to carry them out. For example, before we organized ourselves we didn't have doctors or health promoters. Now, the organization helps us to identify the health promoters among our young people and to train them. Each community makes its own proposals for the projects it wants. Our organization is integrated with all the communities in the region. We do not accept direct government aid. We are autonomous and independent.

We work collectively. When the organizing started, everybody, men and women, started to organize. Women left their homes to go to meetings. They didn't do their work at home anymore. There was no time for that. In the past we never worked collectively like we do now. Men used to tell women that they had no rights. Now we know that we all have rights. Young people work together—men and women together. Our lives are better now. We are happier now because we all have the right to get out of the house, to work in the projects and to participate in the life of our town.

Our organization is also political. We organize for new laws and for our own government. Our goal is to govern ourselves—to be independent and autonomous of the state and federal government. We make our decisions communally and we carry them out. All deci-

---

[10]ARIC: Rural Association of Collective Interest, a campesino organization throughout *Las Cañadas* and the Lacandón jungle. See Chapter 1 for the history of ARIC.

sions here are made at the General Assembly. Every man and woman over the age of 16 votes in the Assembly, and all of us make decisions together. We talk and then we decide. Somebody presents a proposal or raises an issue to the Assembly, and we all talk about it. Some people agree with the proposal. Some people don't agree, so they have to say why they don't agree. When everybody has had an opportunity to speak, then we vote on what to do.

The General Assembly has a leadership council that's called the Local Parliament, and it picks four representatives—a president, an alternate, a secretary and a treasurer—to go to the Regional Parliament.

There are 13 commissions in charge of all the work that needs to be done at the local level, and each commission has representation at the regional level. These are the commissions: 1) Honor and Justice, 2) Women, 3) Youth, 4) Elders, 5) Political Issues, 6) Education, 7) Health, 8) Development, 9) Production and Commercialization, 10) Human Rights, 11) Finances and Taxes, 12) Land and Agrarian Issues, and 13) Labor. If a problem can't be resolved at the local level—some crimes or serious human rights violations, for example—it goes to the regional level. There are four representatives in the Regional Commission. The Regional Commission has all the authority to resolve the problems.

At the Regional Assemblies people from all over this region come to meet, talk and organize—to see how we are going to plan our government. We talk about how we are going to organize, what we are going to do about this or that problem, what we are going to do for the children and how we can improve our situation. We also report on what is happening in our community. Some people have to walk for a day or two to get to the Regional Assembly. Sometimes we meet here, sometimes in another town.

### Women's Organizations
WOMEN SPEAK: We started organizing collectively as women in 1991. That was when we first started to venture out of our homes. It was easier for us women to organize than it was for the men. Our first project in 1991 was the organic garden. We made an agreement

with the men and they prepared the soil for us to plant. We carried black soil and manure, we mixed it all, and we started to work. Not all the women wanted to work, and not all the husbands would allow their wives to work. They said, "Who's going to cook my food if you go out?" Sometimes the woman wanted to work but her husband wouldn't allow her. But some men encouraged their wives to work with us.

Now most of the women work collectively. The men don't say anything bad anymore. It's not like it used to be. We had the organic gardening project, the project to raise chickens and the rabbit project. But in 1995 there was a military invasion, and we had to abandon everything and flee to the mountains. We lost everything then.

Now we have other collective production projects. One of them is the bakery. We have six bakery groups. We still do organic gardening, and we have the chicken project. All the women's groups have a president, a secretary and a treasurer. There is also a general coordinator who oversees all the projects. She checks to see if the groups are working. She sees if the president is merely nagging the women or if she is doing her work.

Our main production project is coffee. We pick the coffee beans together and put them in great big baskets—the way we did with you today. Then we clean the beans well and put them out to dry in the sun. Tomorrow we will count how many sacks of coffee we have. We do all this together, and when we sell the coffee, the money is for all of us. This year the price of coffee is 12 pesos a kilo. The brokers come here to buy. The women have to decide how much each one of us will get, and how much we will use to buy what we need for the project.

We also have a Women's General Commission. We meet once a month, here or in other towns. These meetings are only for women. When all the representatives from all the communities come, there are about 150 of us. We had a meeting to draft the rules of the Women's Commission. We also had a meeting to discuss the Revolutionary Women's Laws. Do you know these laws? These laws are very important. They are teaching us about our rights as women. We think that our lives as women are better now. We are happier now because we have the right to do what we want and need to do. Now even the young girls go out to work with us.

## Education

WOMEN SPEAK: Everybody here is Tzeltal and everybody speaks Tzeltal. Most of the women don't speak Spanish. The children speak Tzeltal with their families. At school they learn only Spanish. That's why if we know a little Spanish, we try to speak with them. Otherwise they won't understand what goes on in the classroom, because the teachers speak only in Spanish.

We have an elementary school here. There are six teachers in the school. They are government teachers and they're not from here. They work only four days a week. They live here during those days, and then they go back to their hometowns for the weekend.

From 1994—after the uprising—until 1996, the children didn't go to school. The school was closed for almost two years. We didn't have teachers, and the children weren't learning anything. After long negotiations with the Chiapas Department of Education, we accepted government teachers, but only under our own conditions: that they work hard and teach the children. We've had teachers again now, since September 1996.

A SCHOOLTEACHER SPEAKS: Yes, I am a teacher here. I can tell you about the school. The school building was built in 1972. Between January 1994 and October 1996 it wasn't functioning. What happened is that when the conflict started in January 1994, the teachers got scared and left. The teachers were not from this town. They were from Comitán and from other towns of Chiapas. They were afraid of the war. They were afraid that this village would get attacked. So they left, and for two years the children didn't go to school. The community tried to look for teachers. Finally, the state government hired teachers. The teachers come from the Chiapas Department of Education. In October 1996 the school reopened.

The academic level of the children was very low. The children who were supposed to be in third grade couldn't read or write. During the two years without schooling, they had forgotten everything they'd learned before. Now, we're starting from the beginning, teaching the basics. The children are very excited to learn. They're very motivated. It's a sacrifice for them to attend regularly because they're very poor and they need to help their parents in the fields, but they still come to school everyday. There are six teachers in the school. We have about 120 students. In first grade alone, there are 90 children. All of us are new teachers, and this is our first teaching experience. We come from San Cristóbal and from Tuxtla. We love to work here. It's a great place. The people are very nice to us, and they treat us very well. We live right here in the school and go home for the weekend.

*b.* **The Military Offensive of January 1994**

*Following the Zapatista uprising of January 1, 1994, the Mexican Army moved quickly to retake the cities that the Zapatistas had occupied: Ocosingo, Altamirano, Las Margaritas and San Cristóbal de las Casas. This was complete and total war against the Zapatistas with the strategy of eliminating them militarily. It lasted 12 days. As the Zapatistas retreated into the jungle, however, the only place that the two armies actually clashed was in Ocosingo. After the battle, 30 bodies of civilians and EZLN combatants were found with signs of torture and extrajudicial execution. Local people also stated that they had seen a mass grave with a dozen incinerated bodies.*

*On January 14, former US Attorney General Ramsey Clark led a fact-finding mission to Chiapas. In his report, he stated that these kinds of serious human rights violations occurred not only in Ocosingo, but also in San Cristóbal, Chanal, Oxchuc, Altamirano and in many communities of the jungle.[11] Communities were bombed, and many people suspected of collaborating with the Zapatistas were imprisoned, harassed, beaten or disappeared. In the jungle, entire communities abandoned their villages as the Army arrived.*

*Although many villages were searched and occupied by the Army in January 1994, Morelia—part of the Altamirano municipality— stands out as a particularly notorious case in which human rights of*

---

[11]*El alzamiento* (Mexico: La Jornada Ediciones, 1994)

*civilians were violated. Below, the people of Morelia narrate what happened in their town:*

### The Invasion of Our Town

WOMEN SPEAK: Things were quiet here after the uprising of January 1. Then on January 7, the Army came into town. They came very early, at about six in the morning. Our husbands had already gone to the fields, but the women were still in our homes. The soldiers came into the houses. They broke down the doors and destroyed everything. They harassed the women. They broke into our houses yelling, "Get out of the house! I want to see if your husband has anything here! We know you are all Zapatistas!"

They pushed us out of our homes into the street, and they went into the house to search. They said they were looking for weapons. They threw everything out of our houses. The soldiers asked us, "Where are you hiding the weapons? Where are you hiding the guerrillas?" We told them, "Why don't you look in the mountains? Why do you come to the communities to look? We don't even have money to buy food. How could we buy weapons?"

If the soldiers found a man in the house, they pushed him outside. They tied the men up and took them to the basketball court. They pushed all the men to the ground and made them lay there for hours. They beat them and tortured them. When it was all over, three men had disappeared, and we couldn't find them. We looked for them in the jail and at the hospital in Altamirano. One of them was an old man who was sick with fever. They dragged him out of his house and took him away in a car. We had no idea where they had taken him or the others. After two months we found their dead bodies—only their bones really—in the ravine by the river. They had been tortured and then killed by the Army. We recognized the bodies by their clothes.

Twenty-three men were also taken away in the helicopters at night. We were so worried about them. We didn't know how they were, where they had taken them, or if they were going to kill them. They were finally able to return after a long time. The women were sad. They kept saying, "Why did the Army come? We've committed no crime. We're not doing anything bad."

A MAN SPEAKS: When the Army came into Morelia they took me in the helicopter, along with the other men. The judicial police interrogated me. They accused me of being in the Zapatista Army because I have strong legs and strong arms. They said that proved that I had military training. But it's by working in the fields that your arms get strong. I had an insect bite on my thigh that got infected. They said that was proof that I lived in the jungle. They tortured me. They hit me on the back with a piece of wood. Some of the men were tortured with electric shocks. Another man's face was all swollen  because of the beatings. I was in *Cerro Hueco* State Prison in Tuxtla Gutiérrez for two months. I received legal counsel from the Fray Bartolomé Human Rights Office. Finally, I got out of jail when the paraffin test proved to the government that I had not used a firearm.

A HUMAN RIGHT'S WORKER SPEAKS:[12] The Mexican Army claimed they did not commit human rights violations during the Chiapas war of January 1994. But serious violations were committed in Morelia where the Mexican Army tortured and executed three civilians, and tortured other civilian non-combatants. These violations have been denounced by the Inter-American Human Rights Court.[13]

We arrived in Morelia on January 13 when we were finally able to enter with the Mexican Caravan to bring aid. The people were terror-stricken. Three men had disappeared. Twenty-three people had

---

[12]The human rights worker, who has asked to remain anonymous, was part of the Mexican Caravan for Peace that toured indigenous communities in *Las Cañadas* and the rainforest in January 1994 to observe and report on human rights violations and to bring humanitarian aid to displaced populations.

[13]After a careful investigation, the Inter-American Human Rights Court of the Organization of American States formally accused the Mexican Federal Army of committing crimes against humanity—including execution and torture of civilian non-combatants—in the village of Morelia, Chiapas, in January 1994.

been taken away by the Army in helicopters. We didn't know where the Army had taken them. It turned out that some of the men had been taken to Comitán, and others had been taken to the *Cerro Hueco* State Prison. They had been tortured on the way to jail. The remains of the three men that the Army killed were found many days later in the ravine area between Morelia and Altamirano. Although it was the National Human Rights Commission that first gathered the remains, the Mexican Army took the bodies away from them. The Army argued that the remains needed to be analyzed by their military medical experts. But the Army did more than just analyze. When the remains were returned, the bones were all mixed-up in a box. You couldn't tell whose bones were whose.

Then an international forensic anthropology team came to work on the remains. It was a team that had worked in Argentina and Guatemala exhuming clandestine cemeteries. They were able to put the bones together again. They fixed them all perfect. Finally the remains were returned to the families in Morelia for burial.

### c. The Second Military Offensive, February 1995

*After the first 12 days of war in 1994, national and international pressure rose in favor of negotiations with the Zapatistas, and Mexican President Carlos Salinas called for an end to the Army offensive. The last thing the Mexican government wanted as NAFTA was beginning to take effect, was to present an image of a Mexico at war or a Mexico too unstable for foreign investment. Reluctantly, the government agreed that negotiations with the rebels would be necessary.*

*Between January 1994 and February 1995, however, while the Mexican government gave lip-service to the idea of negotiations, it was simultaneously training its army for a different kind of war. The United States—interested in preserving stability for its business interests in Mexico—proved to be a loyal ally and chief adviser. US military aid to Chiapas, in the form of weapons, material and training, increased by leaps and bounds after 1994. More commercial arm sales were approved to Mexico,*[14] *and the infamous US Army School of the Americas began training Mexican officers in unprecedented numbers.*[15] *While much of US aid has been disguised as anti-narcotics training, it appears that the great majority of it has been directed to counter-insurgency efforts. With US training and support, the Mexican government strategy began to change in 1995 from one of eliminating the Zapatistas militarily to one of "low-intensity warfare," aimed at eroding the Zapatista civilian bases of support in Chiapas and around the country.*[16]

*A second Army offensive into Zapatista territory took place in February 1995 in direct violation of the ceasefire. This offensive laid the foundation for the beginning of the low-intensity warfare strategy. The communities of the Lacandón rainforest experienced the brunt of the 1995 offensive, with the dismantling of the* aguascalientes *at Guadalupe Tepeyac and incursions into other communities. But Morelia, in the region of* Las Cañadas *was also one of the villages where the Mexican Army entered. What happened in February 1995 is related by the townspeople.*

### Forced to Flee

WOMEN SPEAK: On February 9, 1995, the Army came into town again. They came in near where the *aguascalientes* is now. But we found out in time. We were told that the Army was coming—that

---

[14]Low-intensity warfare is a strategy the United States has employed in Central America and now Mexico. A post-Vietnam alternative to committing large numbers of troops in an all-out war, it is a long-term strategy of harassment, intimidation and economic strangling of the civilian bases of support for an insurgency.

[15] Between 1996 and 1998, the US State Department approved over $360 million in licenses for Direct Commercial Sales (DCS) of defense equipment to Mexico. (S. Brian Wilson. www.globalexchange.org/campaigns/mexico/slope).

[16]In the first two years after the Zapatista uprising, the School of the Americas trained as many Mexican officers as it had in the previous 48 years (S. Brian Wilson. www.globalexchange.org/campaigns/mexico/slope). And by 1997, 35.7% of all students at the US Army School of the Americas were from Mexico (Adam Isacson and Joy Olson, *Just the Facts,* Latin American Working Group, 1999, p. 91). The School of the Americas has been accused of training Latin American officers in torture, psychological warfare and targeting civilian populations.

they were close. So, when the Army got here they found an empty town. The only ones here were the PRI people. There are about twenty PRI people here. When the Army came, the PRI people didn't talk. They didn't tell the Army where we were or where we went. That's why we have a good relationship with the PRI people now, because they didn't talk.

We fled immediately. We didn't wait, because we had already seen what kinds of things the Army does. We fled with nothing but our suffering. We lived in the mountains, in the forest. We were cold, because we didn't have enough clothes. We didn't have food or blankets—nothing. How could we carry our things when we had to flee with our children? There were 10 children in some families! The children were cold and hungry. We could stand it, but not the children. They suffered much more than we did. We hid in the mountains for about three months. People from another village helped us by giving us food for the children.

When we came back, the soldiers had gone and the town was empty. But we knew they'd been here because there was corn spilled all over the floor of our houses. They threw everything around. We had nothing to eat. We didn't have our cornfields. Well, who was going to plant corn when all the men had fled? We picked some of the coffee that was left in the fields, and we sold it to buy a little food. There was no corn or beans to eat. We went hungry for a whole year, because we hadn't planted. We can still see some of the signs of malnutrition in our children even now. They had to go hungry for too long. Now, for the first time since we came back, we are finally being able to harvest a little corn and beans.

When we came back, we couldn't leave town because the Army was patrolling the roads. The soldiers are still there. They are all over, in many places around here. It's dangerous for us women to go to the cornfields alone. But we have to go to the fields! We have to get firewood! The Army is always coming to our town to bother us. Many women get discouraged and don't want to work. They say, "The Army will come again, and we'll have to flee and we'll lose what we've worked on."

We have organized in this way—in an autonomous community—

so that we can have better lives. The government promises to help us, but they are only words. If we make demands of the government it is only because we have nothing. We are suffering with our children. We are demanding changes because all the indigenous people everywhere are suffering.

We have the following demands. We want the Army to leave and stop harassing our communities. We want the war against us to be stopped. We want the government to honor the San Andrés Accords, which they signed. We want our rights as Indians to be respected. And we want to be treated like all Mexicans and like all human beings—with respect and dignity—so that we can develop our communities and manage our own lives.

This is what we think. If we organize, we will get what we need. If not, who will give it to us? If we don't search, we won't find it. If we don't struggle, it won't be there for us.

### 2. Oventik: Voices from the Highlands

"Welcome to Oventik! Please feel free to do what you want. This is your home and you are free here. You can walk around, you can talk to people, you can run, you can have fun, you can dance, you can sing." —Zapatista commander

*In the early morning of the last day of 1995, our small group of family and friends (four adults and my three teenage children) arrived in Oventik, the Zapatista cultural center in the highlands of Chiapas. The day before, we had been running around in San Cristóbal, getting the accreditation documents from Mexican and US independent organizations that recommended us as trustworthy people. After a thorough check at the front gate, we got in and dropped our bags on the dirt floor of the hut that would serve as our dormitory. Then we turned to shake the hand of the tiny guerrilla commander. He wasn't any taller than my 12-year-old son. He wasn't any taller than I am—and I am a very short woman! "Welcome to this special place called an aguascalientes," he said. "Welcome to Oventik! Please feel free to do what you want. This is your home and you are free here. You can walk around, you can talk to people, you can run, you can have fun, you can dance, you can sing."* This was the first time I had ever been in Zapatista territory, and it was the first time I had ever talked to a guerrilla comandante. *We had come for the festivities of the second anniversary of the Zapatista uprising. That night we witnessed the celebration, and we danced, together with the thousands of Mayan Tzotzil people who had come in from all over the highlands of Chiapas.*

*They started to arrive early that evening—entire families of men, women and children, all wearing the traditional clothing of their towns.* They also wore red bandannas over their faces, symbolically indicating their identity as civilian Zapatistas. The festivities began at nightfall with lights, fireworks and music. A ceremony followed where young men and women assembled in front of the Mexican flag and the EZLN comandantes.*

*After the ceremony there was the fiesta, and in typical Zapatista fashion, people danced all night long.* "La del moño colorado/ ya me tiene tan mareado," *the musicians sang to the tune of their marimba, long after we had gone to bed. In the early morning, the families started their long trek uphill out of the aguascalientes, pouring onto the highway to catch rides on pick-up trucks and vans or to walk back to their communities. The children were sleepy, clinging to their mothers' backs or shuffling along behind their fathers. The young women's hair was not as perfectly arranged as the night before, and many of them had lost their beautiful ribbons. Some men and women no longer wore their bandannas.*

*Still, there was something special about this party—something fun and clean and exciting that I couldn't quite define at the moment. Later, I realized what it was. We've been at so many indigenous parties in the many years we have lived in Guatemala and Chiapas, but at this one, people had enjoyed themselves in an environment of respect for one another. There had been no alcohol, no fights, and no harassment of women. I thought then that these fiestas are a symbol of the Zapatista movement and of the indigenous people of Chiapas. They are decent, respectful, fun-loving and disciplined.*

*This was my first encounter with civilian Zapatistas. I wanted to learn as much as possible about who these people were, what their goals were, their objectives, their dreams. Like many Mexicans and international visitors, I wanted to know more about the indigenous people's movement for civil rights that was being staged in this southeastern corner of Mexico.*

*Almost a year and half later, in April 1997, I had the following conversation with five Zapatista civilians in Aguascalientes 2, the Cultural Center of Oventik. They talked with me about their lives, what the Zapatista movement has meant for them, the effects of the war in their communities, and the changes that Zapatista ideals have brought to the lives of men and women.*

### Stories from Oventik[17]

### Our Lives, Our Childhood, Our Education, Our Work

JOSEFA: My childhood was very sad because my parents were poor. As a girl I had many problems. One of them was my lack of education. I never had the opportunity to go to school to learn to read and write. In those days there were already rural schools, but the schools were far away and I was not allowed to go alone. I would have had to walk for an hour and a half, so I didn't go to school.

MARCELA: I went to school for only a few days. This wasn't enough to learn anything. Also, the teachers were no help. They weren't good teachers. They were there because the government sent them, but they weren't interested in teaching Indians. The children were always playing. It was as if there was no teacher. Many of us wanted to learn more, but we had no money to continue with school.

LUISA: I never went to school. It was too far away. Everything I know, I learned from my parents. My parents gave me a different type of education. They talked to me about how a young woman

---

[17]Interview with five Mayan Tzotzil people who are members of the Zapatista civilian support base. Held in the Oventik *Aguascalientes* on April 10, 1997.

ought to be. They said I had to behave. They told me that there are honest people, but also that there are bad people, who could treat me bad and hit me. My parents taught me the art of weaving and making cloth. They taught me to make handwoven baskets. My parents were artisans.

CARLOS: We suffered a lot when I was a child. We suffered because we had no resources, and we couldn't improve our lives. When I was a child, I went hungry a lot. I learned to read and write a little, but it was hard because I had to walk far away to go to school. My parents taught me how to work. They taught me how to prepare the soil to cultivate corn and beans. I learned to carry firewood. I learned many things from my parents. My father taught me to be an honest man like him.

GERMAN: I only learned a little. I didn't finish elementary school because my family didn't have money. The days I was in school, I didn't learn very much. The public school teachers didn't want to teach us. They go to the schools, but they don't do their duty of teaching. There are rural schools, but we had no money to continue studying. We also want our children to get an education, but we have no resources to send them to school.

### The Zapatista Movement
GERMAN: We are Zapatistas now. We got started in the struggle by organizing. Our community representatives explained to us what the movement is all about. We learned that the situation had to change, because we could no longer live as we had been living. When we became Zapatistas, we realized that we are people, that we are persons, that we are human beings who need to be treated as such. We have never been treated as human beings by the government or by the *ladino* people, by the *kashlanes*.

Then we started to participate in the struggle, both men and women. We have our representatives now. Women also have their own representatives. In the assemblies, men and women participate, work and struggle together.

This is how we understand it: that if we all work together we can change our situation; that if we struggle together, our cause will triumph someday. This is our hope as Zapatistas. But this struggle isn't only for us. It's a struggle for justice for all men and women in Chiapas and Mexico, and for all the people of the world. Our struggle is for everybody. We have always been very clear when we say that this *aguascalientes* is not for the people of Oventik. This *aguascalientes* is for the people of the world. People from every nation have come here, and we receive them with open arms. They come here because they believe in our struggle.

We have this hope for all men and women of the world: We hope that here in Chiapas, we will achieve victory for everybody.

### The War

JOSEFA: There is increased military presence in the highlands now, particularly around Oventik. The militarization causes many problems for us women. With the military bases so close to our communities, we can't go to work anymore because of the presence of the soldiers. We don't know what could happen. We never know what the Army is going to do. What the government wants to do is to take over our *aguascalientes* cultural center. They know it's an important place for the Zapatistas. We don't know what day or at what time we'll have to flee to avoid more deaths and more confrontations.

LUISA: I'm worried. I can't go out to collect wood with my children. I can't go to sell my weavings. We need the income we get from our weavings; we sell them to buy our food. But our main concern is that if the Army comes by surprise, there will be many deaths. We have many children, and we can't run as easily with children. If they surprise us, they could kill us all. That's my concern.

JOSEFA: Women are afraid. When people have to flee, the men run faster than the women. When men go out to work in the fields, the women are alone in their homes and we can be attacked by surprise. If there is a military offensive and the Army tries to take Oventik, the women will suffer. We don't know when our enemy will come. We don't know if they will come during the day or at nighttime. The whole community is ready to leave at any moment. We are organized. We are ready to flee with everything we own. We are ready to flee with our children.

CARLOS: It is very difficult to be a Zapatista. It's a long and hard struggle. Our struggle is for all the indigenous *campesinos*. We have been struggling for three years already, and the situation is getting worse for us. The Army surrounds us and is constantly trying to provoke us. They harass us because we are Zapatistas. We can't do our work, and we can't go to the fields. The government isn't interested in peaceful solutions to end the war. It's not interested in negotiating. They want to destroy us. The people in our communities are suffering from lack of food and medicines. We are persecuted by the government because we are civilian Zapatistas, and because we are the representatives of our communities.

### Zapatista Women
LUISA: Life was very different before. In the old days the man felt that he had to control his wife. He didn't permit her to talk to another person, let alone dance. That was our culture. Not very good, but it was like that. In the old days, if a woman looked at another person, her husband would get jealous and beat her up. It was terrible! It still happens today. We know it still happens. But it's against the law now, and that is the big difference. If a man mistreats his wife or another woman, this is not accepted by the community, and he must be punished. He can't get away with it. It has changed.

Now people dance. Some women dance with their husbands. Other women dance with their relatives or close friends. The single women dance with single young men. Some women don't like to dance with men, so they dance with their girlfriends. Dancing was not part of our culture before. What we do now—men and women dancing together—that wasn't done before. Not even men danced in social dances. Only the men who had *cargos*[18] danced, and they only danced for religious rituals, when they performed religious plays. But we never had dances for everybody like we do now. Why did it change? Well, our organization is always changing. I think it's better, not worse. But people don't understand the changes sometimes and they get confused. We have to analyze everything—what's important to do, what we *can* do. We have to analyze whether the changes we propose are going to work out, or if they're going to end up hurting people, the community or the family. If it's going to hurt instead of help, then we shouldn't do it. But if it's going to help, then we should do it, even if it's difficult. The changes related to women's rights are especially hard for the men because they don't understand. It's only when we understand, when we know that life cannot continue as it has been and that it has to change, that the situation gets better. Men start to understand these changes through the support and explanation of the representatives of each community.

There have been changes in the families as well—not every family, but most of them. Now men and women talk about how they are going to work. They have to think, and they ask one another about their work. In the past the man went to work, and he didn't say where or how far he was going. All he did was ask for his *tortilla* and *pozol*,[19] and out he went, without saying goodbye to his family. Now it has changed. When the husband is ready to prepare the soil, he asks his wife about the best place to plant. He listens to her words. He pays attention to her counsel now. Little by little the lives of people are changing. Their lives are improving.

---

[18] A *cargo* is a religious position in the traditional Indian Catholic syncretic church. Some of the religious *cargos* involve caring for the saints or images in the church, being a member of the religious brotherhoods, or taking care of the *fiestas* or traditional religious celebrations. There are also *cargos* that are positions of political leadership that are assigned in community assemblies. In this conversation, the term refers to a role played in the traditional religious celebrations. People with *cargos* wear masks and dance, usually acting out a play or traditional story.

[19] Pozol is a drink made of cornmeal.

MARCELA: For the Zapatista women, the Revolutionary Women's Laws are very important. They are important for all indigenous women because these laws say that women must be respected as persons. We have the same rights as all Mexican women and we can't be discriminated against. We have always been discriminated against and we still are. We suffer discrimination from men, from the *caciques* in the communities, and from the government. How much discrimination do we have to suffer as women? These laws are important. They say that we women have the right to make our own decisions and to take part in agreements. We have the right to defend ourselves as humans. This is the first time in our history that there are laws specifically for women. So, things have changed for women. Now we have opinions. We participate in decision-making and we make agreements at community meetings. It was never like this before. In the past only men went to the meetings.

But we still have a long way to go. Our thoughts and our ideas are still very small because we had no schooling. Our thoughts reflect that we can't think clearly yet. We can't say exactly how to develop the community. We still don't know how to speak and how to make decisions. There are still many things that need to change; there is still much to do. We need women to become aware of what is happening. We want to develop our thoughts and our ideas. We want more participation from women in our general assemblies. We hope that little by little our participation will grow.

LUISA: The Women's Laws are not functioning yet. We have hopes that they will be applied soon. They are going to benefit not only Zapatista women, but all women. We will be able to defend ourselves from our families, from our husbands and from other people. In the past, and even now, women were discriminated against, mistreated and beaten up by their own husbands. That's why the laws are important, because then we women can defend ourselves.

### 3. San José del Río/La Realidad: Voices from the Rainforest

#### a. San José del Río

Our small group of international journalists and human rights observers arrived in San José del Río at about four in the morning. A group of peace campers of different nationalities—mostly Mexican and European—came out to meet us. We had been traveling all night, and the steaming hot coffee and freshly baked bread they gave us tasted delicious. San José del Río was the last stop before our destination—the town of La Realidad. We sat in the small but comfortable cottage eating our breakfast and chatting with the peace campers, just as the sun came out and the village came alive. We learned that the community was in the process of building a clinic and an elementary school. Before we left, still early that morning, everybody was busy at work.

A few days later, I was able to have a conversation with two representatives of San José del Río. At the time of my interview with them, I learned that San José was in the process of becoming an autonomous community. They told me that autonomy was a serious decision for a community—a decision that would affect the way they related to their neighboring communities and to the Mexican State.

Doubtless, that would be true. Until very recently, most people in the rural areas of Chiapas—and throughout Mexico—belonged to one political party, the official PRI party. People tended to follow the policies set by local authorities and party bosses without challenging them, even if the policies were corrupt, oppressive or in detriment to the people's well-being. There was very little political disagreement among rural communities because there were few political choices to disagree about. When opposition political parties and rural organizations appeared in Chiapas demanding greater participation and respect for civil rights, the resulting political diversity brought a more democratic environment to the indigenous communities. But that was also accompanied by a greater degree of disagreement and conflict.

*Communities that have chosen to be autonomous Zapatista communities have united to challenge the government, demand basic human rights and insist on their political and economic sovereignty as Indian peoples. These communities separate themselves from other indigenous communities that are still in agreement with government policies and wait passively for government handouts. Autonomous communities also demand a new relationship with the Mexican State, a relationship based on respect, independence and sovereignty.*

### The History of our Community[20]

MEN AND WOMEN: I'm going to tell you the story of our grandparents. This village, San José del Río, is only about 17 years old. Our grandparents founded this town. It was a plantation before—a *finca* called *El Peten Chayabes*. Our grandparents were day laborers on the *finca*. They worked for the plantation owner for many years—most of their lives. Then, they were able to buy a little piece of land from the plantation. It wasn't the entire plantation, only 160 hectares of hills and stone fields. So, this is our town: it's very little, very bad land. We can't cultivate coffee on this piece of land. We have to go far away from here to grow our coffee.

Our grandparents were not good at organizing. They didn't know how to organize a meeting. They were ashamed of themselves because they couldn't speak very well in Spanish. They only knew how to work for the plantation owner. That's all they knew. But they decided to start organizing to buy better land and to get credit from the government. They asked for credit in a peaceful manner. They asked in a humble manner for services from the government. But they received no solution to their problems. That's why we live on this small bit of rocky land.

Years later, we also asked government institutions for credit. We went to the *INI*, the National Indigenous Institute. We went to the CNC, the National *Campesino* Coalition—a *campesino* union managed by the government. We even went directly to the governor of

---

[20]*Collective testimony from interview held with representatives of San José del Río in May 1997. San José del Río became an autonomous community in 1998.*

Chiapas. In 1982 and in 1985, we were able to get credits, but very little. Then, we joined a union of coffee cooperatives so we could get better prices for our coffee.

Now we work independently, and we're trying to start our own cooperative to sell our coffee. We don't have much coffee—only a piece of land here and one on the other side of the hill. But it's good quality coffee, the little bit we have. We have several collective projects for the production of chickens, and pigs and corn. Our cornfield is not very good, though, because our land is hilly and full of stones.

Politically, we are still in the process of becoming autonomous. We haven't voted for our representatives yet. We have to discuss this process of autonomy with the other neighboring communities. We have to think about it collectively in a very clear manner. After all, autonomy is a very serious decision, and we want to do it right.

### b. La Realidad

*Rocibel, Bealuz, Daudilia, Delfi and Maricela. Four teenage women and one young woman in her thirties sat on the ground around my tape recorder, under the shade of the tree that protected us from the tropical heat of the early afternoon. A few steps away an old woman sat on a stump on her front porch, stitching away at embroidered napkins with Zapatista slogans and designs of masked guerrilla commanders.*

*The tanks and Army trucks would be passing by soon. That meant that these women and all the other women around this part of town would go into their houses. The men would turn their backs to the soldiers, and the children would run and hide. All the young peace campers, on the other hand, would come out with their cameras for a pictorial record of the daily passing of the Army.*

*I had been waiting for this interview for several days, in this my second visit to La Realidad. Other journalists came to this Lacandón rainforest town for an interview with Subcomandante Marcos, or for a photograph of other* comandantes. *My interest, however, was to talk with the townspeople—to learn from them what it is like to live in this famous place. La Realidad is the civilian headquarters of the EZLN in the rainforest. It's the place the guerrilla commanders come to when they leave their hiding posts deep in the jungle. My interview was with the representatives of the women's projects.*

*Young people have an important place in leadership here. In La Realidad, as in all the other Zapatista autonomous towns, children become adults at age 14. By age 16, they can become representatives or* responsables. *They follow the Zapatista rule of mandar obedeciendo—to lead by following—which means that they do what the townspeople ask them to do. It also means that their words are not their own. They are merely spokespersons for the community. These leaders are not elected. Rather, they are chosen by the general assembly. Townspeople choose their* responsables *according to their special qualities of responsibility, intelligence and willingness to do hard work. When they are chosen, they have to accept. It is, after all, an honor.*

*Not all the* responsables *are young people. Many of the primary leaders are middle-aged adults who have a long history of activism in the community. They are chosen to lead and to make important decisions. The* ancianos, *or elders, have very important roles in the community as well. They compose the Council of Elders, and their role is to give advice and to educate others about the traditions— about the "way things are done." The* responsables *come to them with the most difficult problems, and with their experience and knowledge, the elders give advice to the younger people. They are wise men and women who know better than most because their eyes "can see into the past," into the history of their people. Even Marcos, the highest military commander of the Zapatista Army, was guided in his work with advice from old Antonio, the prophetic character of Marcos' writings. Antonio explained to him how things are done, why life is the way it is, and how we can struggle to make it better.*

## The Story of La Realidad[21]

YOUNG WOMEN SPEAK: The name of this town is La Realidad. It is the seat of the autonomous municipality San Pedro de Michoacán. The government calls this the Municipality of Las Margaritas. They don't want to recognize it as an autonomous municipality. In fact, the government wants to start new municipalities. This causes many problems. Recently there was a big meeting at another neighboring town with the government people. They had marimba music and a big dance, and all the politicians were there talking. They wanted to convince us that our autonomous municipality was no good and that it would be better to have a new one organized by the government. This would mean a PRI government, because the PRI people believe everything the governor tells them. So, all of us Zapatistas went to the meeting and started yelling at them, saying that they were lying to us. I think this was in the papers and on TV.

We are the women representatives—or *responsables*—for this town. There are six of us for the women's projects and six for the men's projects—12 in all. We take turns being *responsables*. Every six months there is a change. We've been *responsables* for five months now.

All of us were born here in La Realidad. We all are Tojolabal, but we don't speak Tojolabal—only Spanish. Our parents and all the old people speak Tojolabal, but all of us young people have forgotten it because we didn't learn it at school. We only learn Spanish at school. We are all 17 years old, except for one of us who is 33 years old.

The people at the assembly appointed us to be *responsables*. We told them we couldn't do it, that it was too much work. But the people said we had to do it. So we told them we would try, and that we would do our best. The people told us they trusted that we could do our work because all of us are single, and we don't have the responsibilities of a husband or children.

The men who are *responsables* are married men, but the major-

---

[21]*Collective testimony from interview held with* responsables *of La Realidad in May 1997.*

ity of women *responsables* are single. Children here can't participate in the work, but this girl here who is 14 years old can already participate in the commissions. For example, she can help to make tortillas for the workers in the collective projects. Our work as *responsables* is to organize the collective projects. The women have five collective projects: caring for the chickens, making the bread for the community, embroidering the napkins for sale, working in the collective vegetable garden, and caring for the rabbits. The men work together in the community cornfield, which is far away from the town. In the past, we didn't have any *responsables*. It was only after we got organized in and around 1994 that we started doing this. In the past men drank too much and beat up their wives. But things changed for us after 1994 when we organized as Zapatista civilians.

### February 1995

We can tell you what happened in February 1995. On February 9, the Army came into the community of Guadalupe Tepeyác. That was the town where the first *aguascalientes* was and where the National Democratic Convention was held. Thousands of people from all over Mexico came to talk with the EZLN, and we were able to meet them. Guadalupe Tepeyác was an important town for all of us because the first *aguascalientes* was there. That *aguascalientes* was destroyed by the Army. Now, of course, there is an *aguascalientes* here, as well as in four other towns: Morelia, Oventik, La Garrucha and Roberto Barrios.

The Mexican Army took the town of Guadalupe Tepeyác on February 9, 1995, and they destroyed everything that was there for the *aguascalientes*. The people of Guadalupe fled. First they came over here, and then they went over to that mountain that you see over there. They founded the town of Nueva Guadalupe Tepeyác over there on that mountain.

The day after the Army took Guadalupe, they came here with their tanks. The helicopters were going around and around above us. The soldiers came and put their posts here. They said they were going to give us medicines, and they wanted us women to approach them to see. But we said no thank-you, because we're not used to being taken care of by soldiers. We like to take care of ourselves. We told them to leave, to go away. All the women were standing by the church. We yelled at them to go away.

They said, "Come here. We'll give you medicines. Listen, ladies, you don't understand. We've come to help." But then later on they said we were Zapatistas, that we were controlled by the Zapatistas, and that we were whores of the Zapatistas. That's what they said.

The Army came into our houses and we were afraid. They demanded tortillas from us. They tied our cows to their ropes and stole them. That's when we were afraid, and we decided to flee into the mountains. We were afraid they would attack our town. We were only in the mountains for two days, though. We returned because the children were cold and hungry. The women said that we needed to return because the children were suffering, and because we didn't want the Army to take over our town. So, we returned and we put a fence around our town to protect it. We're not going to flee again. This is our town.

When we fled into the mountains, civil society groups from Mexico came to help us. There was a woman I remember whose name was Ofelia Medina.[22] She is a beautiful woman. The children were sick with fever and coughing. Ofelia told us that they were sick because they weren't eating right. She said it would be better if we returned to our town. She said the Mexican civil society would protect us and that they wouldn't let the Army hurt us. Then all the women organized to return. When we came back, we told the soldiers to go away, that the children were afraid of them. We said we didn't need their medicines because we knew how to use medicinal plants—the herbal medicines that our grandmothers taught us how to use. We scolded them for pointing their weapons at the children, and we told them that they must not have any children of their own, because if they did, they wouldn't do such things. They left very angry. They told us that the Zapatistas were fooling us, that there was no such

---

[22]Ofelia Medina is a Mexican actress and activist working on the defense of human rights in indigenous communities in Chiapas and other southern Mexican states.

thing as civil society, and that it was the foreigners who were manipulating us.

Now, after all these years, the Army is still around here. They come every day to harass us. It's hard for us to go gather firewood because the Army is there, bothering us. Their helicopters fly over us everyday. The other day we were having a meeting and the helicopter flew over us very low. It went around three times.

The government has not honored the San Andrés Accords, although it signed them along with the EZLN. The government made promises but they have not fulfilled what they promised. They are accusing the EZLN of not honoring the accords, but that's a lie. This is the way the government does things; they go to the peace talks, write their agreements, and sign them with no intention of honoring them. This is what we see.

## Peace Campers

The peace campers are young people from Mexico and from all over the world who come here to help us. They make sure the Army doesn't attack us like they did in 1995. When they hear the Army trucks coming down the road, they all come running out to watch. They take photographs, and they write in their notebooks how many Army trucks and soldiers and tanks and helicopters pass by.

If they weren't here, who would care about us? Who would document what the Army does to us? These young people are very brave. They are very nice. They are the civil society of Mexico and of other countries. Sometimes we talk with them and we have nice conversations. They help us carry wood when we come back from the forest. They go with us to make sure that the soldiers don't harass us. So, we help them in whatever way we can, too. We share our *tortillas* with them when we can.

# FOUR

# Paramilitary Wars in Northern Chiapas

# THE STRATEGY OF PARAMILITARY WAR

Having laid the foundations for the low-intensity war through the February 1995 offensive, the Mexican military established numerous outposts and checkpoints near communities of Zapatista influence and began to make its presence felt directly and indirectly. Direct actions have included vigilance and control over travel in and out of the communities, threats and provocations, occasional violent incursions into communities, harassment of women and a few programs here and there, and distributing goods and services to win people over to the government side. Clandestine military activity has been even more nefarious as the Mexican Army has joined with local and state officials to create, train and arm paramilitary groups.

The objective of this kind of low-intensity warfare is to eliminate the Zapatistas without undermining Mexico's already shaky image as a "modern democracy." The fact that the great majority of Zapatista followers are unarmed indigenous civilians means that it is impossible to destroy the Zapatistas militarily without committing massive human rights violations. Therefore, the paramilitary groups have been created and armed to do the Mexican Army's dirty work for them. The current paramilitary violence in Chiapas is a deliberate effort on the part of the Mexican government and its US advisers to try to weaken Zapatista support while distancing themselves from the human rights violations that are a necessary part of their strategy. Ironically, while trying to preserve Mexico's image as a modern democracy, they undermine the foundations of real democracy.

In this new phase of the low-intensity war, the Mexican military, along with various manifestations of the PRI party, have exploited existing community divisions and created others in order to build a context for violence against Zapatista supporters. Groups loyal to the PRI have been trained, armed and encouraged to attack their neighbors who may support other political parties or be sympathetic to the Zapatista cause. "Low-intensity" war is anything but low-intensity for its victims. To date, paramilitary groups like these have murdered hundreds of people and caused tens of thousands of indigenous people to leave their homes.

## Northern Chiapas

This kind of violence manifested itself first in the rural areas of northern Chiapas in 1995, as organized paramilitary groups began to push hundreds of indigenous Chol *campesinos* from their communities. Political, economic, ethnic and religious divisions have contributed to the conflict, which is rooted in an unfair distribution of wealth and land. It is clear, however, that this violence is part of the government's war against civilians who are affiliated with opposition political parties or with the Zapatistas.

Northern Chiapas is a rich agricultural and cattle-raising region dominated and controlled in large part by powerful political bosses called *caciques*, large landholders, and cattle ranchers associated with the PRI. Until recently, ranchers and *caciques* have been supported by the state and federal governments, receiving commercial benefits, political backing, and even paramilitary training in return for their support of the PRI.

In the 1970s, the influence of the local *caciques* and ranchers was challenged as independent groups began to organize to defend their agrarian rights, take over fallow lands, form new *ejidos*, and demand credit and land from the government. These groups sprang up throughout Chiapas, but particularly in the northern region, in the municipalities of Ocosingo and Altamirano, and in the Lacandón forest.

In the 1990s, several groups aligned themselves with the center-left Democratic Revolution Party (PRD) to run for office and gain political power in the municipalities. After the January 1994 Zapatista uprising, this opposition movement grew even more and took on the Zapatista demands as its own. Entire communities and groups throughout Chiapas became part of the Zapatista civilian bases of support. Many Zapatista supporters continue to be members of the PRD, while others have organized as *autónomos,* meaning they no longer participate in any political party, but instead consider themselves civilian Zapatistas.

## "Paz y Justicia"

Beginning in 1995, local PRI-affiliated groups of *caciques* and ranchers organized into armed paramilitary groups in northern Chiapas and then systematically attacked, persecuted, intimidated and killed organized *campesinos*, PRD party members and Zapatista civilians. One such paramilitary group—ironically named Desarrollo, Paz y Justicia, or "Development, Peace and Justice"—started as a PRI development organization and then turned into an armed group. "Paz y Justicia," as it is often called, has leveled sustained attacks against independent PRD and Zapatista civilians in the municipalities of Tila, Sabanilla, Tumbala and Salto de Agua in the northern part of the state. Their attacks have resulted in the eviction of hundreds of Chol *campesinos*, the murders of dozens of people, and continuous attacks on entire villages.[1]

### The Long Walk to Tuxtla

During 1996 and 1997, several indigenous Mayan Chol people who tried to defend their homes and families from these attacks were charged with crimes and sent to the Cerro Hueco State Prison in Tuxtla Gutiérrez. In protest, a contingent of Chol *campesinos* broke through a Paz y Justicia blockade in northern Chiapas and marched across the state to Tuxtla Gutiérrez in April 1997. During April, May, June and July, they camped on the steps of the state government building, demanding freedom for their unjustly jailed relatives, restitution for their material losses, a guaranteed safe return to their communities, respect for their human rights, and an end to the abuses of Paz y Justicia.

Paz y Justicia continued to harass, intimidate, and attack opposition leaders in northern Chiapas, even as the several hundred representatives of the displaced kept up their protests on the steps of the state government building.

During the weeks of the sit-in, I had the opportunity to talk with the protesters about their lives. The following testimonies from both

---

[1]See *México: Deberes incumplidos,* Human Rights Watch/Americas Report on Mexico, April 1997.

# Northern Chiapas/*El Norte*

men and women tell the story of the low intensity war that is still going on in the communities of Tila and Sabanilla in northern Chiapas. They describe the situation in northern Chiapas from 1995 to 1997.

## *Stop the Violence! Stories from the Tuxla Sit-in*

### *1. Tila: Attacks against Community Leaders*

#### *a. Margarita's Story*

*When I started interviewing displaced people from Tila and Sabanilla at the sit-in in Tuxtla Gutiérrez in the summer of 1997, everybody told me I needed to talk with Margarita Martínez, from El Limar, Tila. Everybody said she would be one of the best spokespeople. I'd gone to Tuxtla several times and I hadn't found her. As a local activist and organizer for the displaced, she went back and forth between the sit-in and her community of El Limar in Tila.*

*Finally, I met her in early June at the Women's State Forum in San Cristóbal de las Casas, where she went as a representative of Tila. "That woman over there is Margarita," somebody told me. I saw a woman who looked very different from the other indigenous women present at the forum, who were dressed in their traditional Mayan clothing. In fact, Margarita—with her "punk" urban look— broke all the stereotypes I ever had of what a young Mayan woman was supposed to look like. She is a large, heavy Chol woman with very short hair shaved at the sides, and she wore tattered blue jeans and a loose-fitting old T-shirt. To use her own words, Margarita is "a very strong woman."*

*We arranged an interview in Tuxtla and when we had a chance to talk, I was impressed with her. I found her sitting in a corner quietly teaching embroidery to three women and one man. Although she seemed very shy, it became apparent to me that she was a leader for both women and men at the sit-in. First she made sure that I talked with the other women, and she helped by translating from Chol to Spanish. Then she told me her story. She sat on a chair talking while her best friend, Luisa, whispered the details that Margarita kept forgetting. This is the story of Margarita and Luisa:*

## "*I am a Very Strong Woman*"[2]

My name is Margarita Martínez, and my friend here is Luisa Hernández. We are from El Limar in Tila. My parents are just poor *campesinos.* I've been doing political work for four years. I do political work and I work with the cooperative store. I've also been working with the church as a catechist for ten years. I am 28 years old, and I'm single. Luisa is 25 years old, and she's also single. We live in the store in Luisa's house. But, now my parents want me to go live with them because they fear for my safety.

The problem in El Limar is the conflict that Paz y Justicia has stirred up against the members of the Democratic Revolution Party (PRD), against the Catholic catechists and against the Zapatista bases of support. There are about 510 of us PRD activists. In other words, half of the town is with the PRD and half is with the PRI. The problems started in 1995—on July 14 to be exact—when the Catholic church was taken over by Paz y Justicia.

First, armed Paz y Justicia members attacked us, took over the Catholic church and locked it. The following day they kidnapped Gustavo Hernández, a catechist. They took him to the cemetery where they tried to kill him. Gustavo says they tied his hands behind his back and beat him up. The person who gave the order to kidnap Gustavo was Diego Vázquez, one of the leaders of Paz y Justicia. The ones who organized the attack against us are people who are under the orders of Congressman Samuel Sánchez. They give these attackers police uniforms and caps and dress them as if they were members of the Security Police. But they aren't policemen. They're members of Paz y Justicia. They are indigenous Chol people who are attacking their own Chol brothers and sisters.

Paz y Justicia members stand at the crossroads outside of town. They won't let us go through, or come into our own communities. They're armed and they attack us. The only thing we want is not to have problems. We want peace. We are asking the government for housing, sewage, and development for our communities. That's all we're asking for. But the people of Paz y Justicia don't agree with us

---

[2]Interview with Margarita Martínez, Tuxtla Gutiérrez, June 1997.

politically. They don't want to allow any party other than PRI. They say it's not good to have other parties. They don't want the Worker's Party (PT), they don't want the Cardenista Front,[3] and they don't want the PRD. They say there should be only one party: the PRI. Many people in our communities have nothing. They don't have a house, they don't have clothes for their children, nothing. So we are starting a peaceful organization to solve these problems. All we want is real peace and real justice. On September 4, 1995, we organized our opposition party.

The kidnappings started in 1994. Paz y Justicia members accused the townspeople of crimes they didn't commit, and people were jailed unjustly. In 1994, Paz y Justicia also attacked the teachers and ran them out of El Limar, because they belonged to opposition parties. Paz y Justicia people are protected by Congressman Samuel Sánchez and by the Municipal President. In other words, these Paz y Justicia people commit crimes and then they act as if they're not doing anything bad. They wash their hands of their crimes and accuse us. They change things around. We also see that when there are problems, the Paz y Justicia people come with the Security Police and the Judicial Police. They come in a convoy, all of them together. That's what I saw last year.

### Catechist and Political Activist

When Paz y Justicia took over the Catholic church, they locked it with three locks. They still don't allow the priest to go in. The catechists started to work again in the community on December 24, but not the priest. There are four catechists in my community. I'm one of them, and Lucia is another one. As catechists, we are very persecuted. We receive death threats. We get ambushed. We can hardly

---

[3]Formerly known as the Socialist Workers' Party, the Cardenista Party is a small party with membership in only a few highland municipalities of Chiapas. It has been discredited for being corrupt, for being co-opted by the PRI and for participating in the formation of paramilitary groups in the area of Chenalho'. The Cardenista Party is not associated with Cuauhtémoc Cardenas, who was the Mayor of Mexico City in 1998 and 1999 and the presidential candidate for the Democratic Revolution Party (PRD) and the Workers' Party (PT) in 2000.

go to our church meetings. We can't go in and out of our community because of these problems.

The Paz y Justicia people don't want to see preachers. They don't want to hear the Word of God. They say that's where the problems started. They blame Bishop Samuel Ruíz and our priest. They say they give us weapons. Can you believe it? We don't have any weapons! Our priest only talks about how we have to love one another. He only preaches the Word of God. We're not like them—only thinking about killing people. They think like that. They want to finish off all the Catholics and all the PRD members. But, they're against us because of our party affiliations, not because of our religion. That's the only reason. We have the same religion. We all believe in God. But their leaders tell them that we're bad, that we are against their religion. That's not true. We're all children of God.

I like to talk about the Word of God. I like what it says—that we have to love the people who have nothing, those who are poor and needy. So at church we don't just preach the Word of God, we also struggle for justice to help the needy. That's the way we think. I work with the church, and I also work in a cooperative store that we have. It's a large store now—very well stocked—and we sell a lot of what is needed in town. Paz y Justicia would like to burn the store because they say that we're making too much. I'm the president of the store. The people from our organization are working together in this project—about 80 people, mostly men. I'm also organizing the women, and we're looking to form a group and buy a corn mill so that all of us can work together. Another project we have is the communal cornfield. Sometimes we get three tons of corn from our field.

Paz y Justicia doesn't want to see people like me—women who fight. My friend Luisa Hernández and I are both fighters, and we're winning! That's what has got the Paz y Justicia people so ashamed—that they're men and they're losing to us. Their organization is not working out. They don't want women to win.

## The Attack

On February 14, 1997, I was attacked and injured by Paz y Justicia people. They sent their white guards[4] to the place where I was staying. I was sleeping at the store in Luisa's house—in a little room that serves as the warehouse for the store. It's a small space—only four by three square meters—but it's very well stocked with rice, sugar, oil, everything we sell. It's part of the house, and that's where Luisa and I were sleeping.

What happened was that at midnight, a thin little man named Adolfo López got into the house through the tin roof. Three other men stayed outside while he went in and waited for him to open the door for them from the inside. Well thank heavens that God is good, and that He helped us! Luisa woke up first. I was sleeping, and, really, I didn't feel a thing. It was raining a little that night. Four of us women were sleeping there: Luisa's mother, her little sister, Luisa and me. There wasn't anyone else.

LUISA SPEAKS: I woke up when a drop of water fell on my face. I opened my eyes quickly and got up in a flash. I saw the man coming, and I got up screaming. He was dressed as security police but he's not a policeman. Margarita got up right away too, but the man went after her with a big knife.

MARGARITA SPEAKS: I was sleeping on the ground on a straw mat. I sat up really quick, but then he grabbed me. I grabbed onto his leg, and I was going to grab his hand, but he had the knife, so I just held him back and tried to take away his knife. Then I grabbed the knife by the sharp side and cut my hand. It went on like that for a while—me, sitting on the ground, grabbing his leg with one hand and his hand with another, trying to get his knife from him. He was only in the room for about 10 minutes. Thank God nothing more happened to me!

He hurt me here, too, on my shoulder. See the scar? I was hold-

---

[4]Here Margarita uses the term *guardias blancas*—or white guards—to refer to the *Paz y Justicia* members.

ing on to him so he passed the knife to his other hand. He was trying to kill me. See? He stabbed me in the back here on the right side near the ribs, and here's my other scar—over here on my shoulder. I moved my head, and the sharp tip of the blade entered over the side of my face here by my eye, too. [Another scar goes from her left eyebrow to her left ear].

When I saw that he hurt my shoulder up here, I let his leg go, and I held him down by his waist like this. I grabbed him with my left arm, because my right hand was injured. So I kept holding the man around his waist. I didn't let him move because I'm strong. Yes, I'm a very strong woman! I always carry the heaviest sacks of coffee—the ones that weigh fifty kilos. I'm stronger than most men, and he wasn't strong. He was a thin, little man. I kept trying to take his knife from him. Thank God I didn't let him chop off my hand! Then he hit his head against the light switch on the wall and the light came on. He threw the knife under the table, opened the door and ran outside.

This man is a member of Paz y Justicia, and all four of the people who came to attack us were from Paz y Justicia. I informed the local Attorney General's Office of what happened, but not much has been done about it.[5]

They attacked me because I'm the best organizer and because I'm a fighter. I'm the one that my male friends like the most—the one they go to when they need help. Diego Vázquez and the people of Paz y Justicia hate me because I'm a strong woman and they hate strong women like me and Luisa. But we can't live in fear of what will happen to us. We can't be afraid.

Our demand as a group is that Paz y Justicia return what they stole from us. We want to be able to work and organize, and we need guarantees for our safety to be able to do this. We want to get from the government what we need and deserve—development for our

---

[5]According to an article by Juan Balboa in *La Jornada*, July 27, 1997, there had been more than 50 police reports filed against Paz y Justicia members in Tila and Sabanilla alone that have never been investigated. Margarita's police report was among those never investigated.

communities. And we want those Paz y Justicia people to leave us alone.[6]

## b. Guadalupe's Story[7]

I am Guadalupe Tórrez, and I come from a small village in Tila called Masolha Shukha. I have a little house there. I have three sons and one daughter now. Two of my children died when they were babies because they became ill and there was no doctor in my town. My oldest son was killed recently.

One of my sons works in Villahermosa, the capital of the state of Tabasco. He sent me money to build my house. I have two other sons who are here at this sit-in in Tuxtla. My daughter is here with me, too.

My two sons who are here were in jail in Cerro Hueco State Prison for many months. When we arrived here and began to protest, they were still in jail, but on May 14, thanks to God and our lawyers, they got out. They never committed any crime! Thank God my sons are free now.

I'm about 50 years old, I think. My husband is about 80. He's much older than I am. I married when I was 14 years old. I had no father and my mother didn't want me to be alone, so she married me to this man. He was already very old. He doesn't work any more. I work. I built my own house. I work in the fields. I plant sweet potatoes, yucca, tomatoes, chilies—whatever there is to eat. I'm used to work. I get up to grind the corn and make tortillas at three in the morning. Then I go to the cornfield. In my house I do everything. I carry the corn. I carry the wood for the fire. The government didn't give me tin roofing for my house. The government didn't give me a latrine. It didn't help me with anything! I built my own house. It's my

---

[6]In July 1999, after several attempts on her life, Margarita gave her testimony to Asma Jahangir, the United Nations Special Rapporteur on Summary Executions. While others who have given testimony have later been assassinated, Margarita is still alive and well—a sign that national and international solidarity has made an impact.

[7]From interviews with Guadalupe Tórrez, May and June 1997.

own. I owe it to my work, not to the government.

On July 4, 1996 my oldest son, Juan Ramírez, left at three in the afternoon with his briefcase and his papers. He had to go out of town because he's a teacher. He wasn't afraid to travel because he hadn't done anything wrong. I never saw him again. My friend told me that she heard in the news that my son had been killed. I asked the Security Police about him, and they said they didn't know where he was. A young man came and said, "Ay! Your son Juan Ramírez is dead. Paz y Justicia people killed him."

My poor son! I don't know why they killed him. He left five daughters. I cry and cry now. His wife and daughters cry too.

Now, in my community of Masolha Shukha we can't go out to work. We can't go to our cornfields. Paz y Justicia men are looking for people out on the roads. They have weapons, and they kill people. I saw how they were bringing their weapons in a car. They killed all the cows my son had, and they ate the meat. They took my horses, too. I had seven good horses to carry wood and to carry the corn. They killed all my pigs. They even killed my dog with a machete.

Now the government says they don't have money to pay us back for our horses and for our cows. Why did they allow Paz y Justicia to do this to us in the first place? We had to work so hard to buy a cow, to build a stable, to build a house. Now we're poorer than we were before. Where are we going to find the money? My grandchildren were used to drinking milk. They were used to having sugar. Now it's not like before, sister. Everything has changed. We have no money to buy food, shoes, or clothing for them.

I'm really angry now! We've been at this sit-in for two months waiting in front of the government building. There are still 46 prisoners—political prisoners—in Cerro Hueco State Prison. We want them all out!

### Salvador Ramírez (Guadalupe's Son)[8]

I am going to talk about my brother Juan Ramírez. On July 4, 1996 we decided to leave our community called Masolha Shukha to

---

[8]From interview with Salvador Ramírez, June 1997.

make our car payments in Villahermosa. My brother and I each have a car that we were buying on credit, and since we were overdue with our payments we decided we'd better go pay so that we wouldn't lose the cars. We asked the Mexican Army for protection because of the political problem we are having in the northern zone of the state. They are problems caused by ideological differences. The people from Paz y Justicia are pressuring us to affiliate with their political party, the PRI, and we don't want to.

We belong to an independent *campesino* organization called *Abushu*—a Tzeltal word that means "night walkers." *Abushus* are little ants that come out at night to look for their food.[9] This organization exists in Tila and other municipalities of northern Chiapas. Paz y Justicia hates us and wants to destroy our organization. They say we are against the government. They hate us because we have struggled against unjust government policies and for the development of our communities. The government has abandoned our communities.

On July 4 my brother Juan, my brother Artemio and I left town with a woman and her children. We left in two cars at three in the afternoon. We got to another town called Miguel Alemán, and we were told we couldn't go through because we were civilians. Paz y Justicia had the road blocked with stones.

We never made it to Villahermosa. Paz y Justicia members pulled us out of our cars and beat us up. You can see the scar I have on my face from those beatings. First they pulled out my brother Artemio. We have already identified the person that hit him. There was no doubt. I saw it all, and I testified. They tried to pull out my brother Juan as well. He ran towards the mountains but they ran after him

---

[9] *Abushu*, like other *campesino* groups in Chiapas, has organized around land tenure rights and other agrarian issues. It negotiates with government institutions for credit, *ejido* titles and development projects for rural communities, and it also organizes direct actions. Landowners accuse *Abushu* of promoting illegal land take-overs. However, *Abushu* claims that the land it takes is either *ejido* or communal land, and therefore belongs to the *campesinos*. Because of such conflicts, *Abushu* has also had to organize to protect its members against the attacks of large landowners, cattle ranchers, *guardias blancas* and other paramilitary forces.

and caught him.

They also held me and fought with me. The Security Police told me to get into the police truck and I was taken to a clinic in El Limar along with my brother Artemio. But my brother Juan was never freed. He was kidnapped and killed by Paz y Justicia right there in the town of Miguel Alemán, which is a Paz y Justicia stronghold.

On the morning of July 5 we went to look for my brother and to recover our cars. They told us that Juan had gone home, and that my car had been taken there as well. This was all a bunch of lies. Up to now neither the vehicles nor the body of my brother have been recovered. Nothing. We know he was killed because there were witnesses who saw the murder.

On the evening of July 4 at about nine o'clock, we had gone to the Public Ministry and denounced the disappearance of my brother and the aggression against us. The Public Ministry accepted our testimony. They said we could go, that we were free, that it was obvious that Paz y Justicia were the aggressors, not us, and that the whole case was going to be investigated. But by the next morning everything had changed. The people from Paz y Justicia said that we had attacked them. They accused us of homicide and destruction of property. We were incarcerated.

I was in Cerro Hueco jail for 10 months without being charged. My brother Artemio was in jail too. The accusations against us were false, and there was never enough evidence to prove them. But they made *us* present evidence to prove our innocence! The case was thrown out, and we are free now. Now they tell us that we never committed any crime. There also was an investigation of the disappearance of my brother Juan. Nothing has been resolved on his case yet, and there hasn't been any compensation for the stolen vehicles.

I read in the paper that Paz y Justicia people are saying they want peace, but this is a lie. Even if Congressman Samuel Sánchez says that he's ready to negotiate, his people are not ready. They continue with the harassment and aggressive acts. The situation of war against the people has not changed in the municipalities of northern Chiapas.

This is what I can tell you. Thank you for listening.

## c. Gloria's Story

I met Gloria—a 30-year-old single mother and a representative of the displaced of Masolha Grande—in early June 1997 at the Women's State Forum in San Cristóbal de las Casas. She had gone there, along with Margarita, as a representative from Tila. I got to know Gloria at the Forum when we participated together in a workshop on violence against women. Later on, I talked with her several times at the sit-in in Tuxtla Gutiérrez. She always sat in a corner with her seven-year-old son. Like Margarita, Gloria was an important leader at the sit-in. This is her story.

### Gloria Torres[10]

My name is Gloria. I am a refugee of Masolha Grande, municipality of Tila. I am a single mother. This is my child. His name is Luis, and he's seven years old. My son wasn't here with me before. He was staying with my mother in my town. My family sent him to be with me when Paz y Justicia said they were going to kill him.

My sister called me and said, "What are you thinking, Gloria? Have you forgotten your child? He was here playing with the other children in the park and some men from Paz y Justicia came to say that they are going to kill him. Unless you don't care about him anymore, I'm going to take him to you right now, because his life is in danger." That's what my sister said to me when she called, and then she brought him over. You see, I'm the main delegate for the displaced from my community of Masolha Grande, and there are constant death threats against me from Paz y Justicia.

On July 15, Paz y Justicia people expelled all of us who are members of the opposition. There are 52 of us displaced from Masolha Grande, and the majority of us are women and children. We went to live in the state of Campeche, northeast of Chiapas, because we have relatives there. Paz y Justicia people were threatening us, and we had to get out of Masolha Grande or we would get killed.

When I was in Campeche I received a letter asking me to come here to a meeting of representatives of the displaced. After that, we

---

[10]Interviews with Gloria Torres, May and June 1997.

all went to another meeting in Jolnixtie [another town in Tila]. I returned to Campeche to tell my people that they could return to Chiapas, but that they shouldn't return to our community, because the situation was still too dangerous there. The thinking right now is that we shouldn't return to our towns, because the government can't guarantee the safety of our people there. So most of us are currently living as refugees in the town of Salto de Agua, and quite a number of people are staying in the Santa Marta Church.

I also refused to return to Masolha Grande, and I'm living in Salto de Agua with my sister. My father told me that the situation continues to be bad in Masolha. He said that people from Paz y Justicia are still buying arms. Congressman Samuel Sánchez gets the arms and he passes them on to Paz y Justicia. That's what my father told me. He also gave me a list of all the people that are still in Masolha who are members of the opposition. They can't get out, and we can't go in.

I'm not going to abandon my friends. We've agreed that we're not returning to our communities until all the political prisoners from our organizations get out of Cerro Hueco State Prison; until they pay us for everything we've lost; and until there's a guarantee for our safe return. That's why I'm not going back. Even though I'm suffering here, I've decided to continue with the struggle.

## 2. SABANILLA: THE CANTINA CONFLICT

### The Story of Jesús Carranza Community[11]

My name is Venancio Vázquez. I represent about 440 people who have been violently expelled from the community called Jesús Carranza by members of Paz y Justicia. I want to tell you from the deepest part of my heart the problems we've had to face in our community.

In years past, there were four *cantinas* in the town of Jesús Carranza that dispensed moonshine illegally. These bars were there

---

[11]From interviews with Venancio Vásquez, Tuxtla Gutiérrez, May 1997.

for about eight or nine years, and townspeople went there every day to drink and to get drunk.

At that time, Micario Pérez was our town councilman. He was a man who really cared about our town, and he requested that the state government close the illegal bars. We supported his efforts as people who care for our community.

What happened then? Well, the four alcohol dealers became like kings—like owners of our town. They decided to get revenge against those of us who were trying to close the bars. Under false accusations from the bar owners, three legally elected town leaders—Micario Pérez, and two other municipal leaders—were put in jail. They were released eventually, after a legal investigation, but by then the bar owners were in control of our town.

These alcohol dealers have power and political connections in the PRI party. They are supported and armed by Samuel Sánchez, a PRI state congressman, and by the mayor of Sabanilla. After they unlawfully jailed our elected leaders, these PRI hard-liners took over the government of our town. Finally, the townspeople got tired of them, and we took over the municipal building in Sabanilla. We wanted the mayor to step down because he wasn't working for the good of the community.

By then, Congressman Sánchez was already organizing Paz y Justicia throughout the northern zone, in the municipalities of Sabanilla, Tila, and Tumbala. Paz y Justicia people have a lot of power and they don't want to share it with anybody. They want the PRI to be the only group with power and control in the communities. So they armed themselves in order to keep their power.

We organized into a peaceful, opposition political party as members of the Democratic Revolution Party. Since 1994, we've also been Zapatista bases of support. The people of Paz y Justicia accuse us of being terrorists, but that's not what we are. On the contrary, we are peaceful people. As you know, it's not a crime to belong to PRD, and it's not a crime to be part of the Zapatista base of support. It's not a crime to be part of the opposition. This is what we are. We are unarmed, peaceful civilians and citizens. We are not terrorists.

On June 19, 1996, Paz y Justicia ran us out of our community, Jesús Carranza. Before then, they'd already been harassing us, shooting at us, threatening us and throwing firebombs. We were always very afraid, especially at night. We weren't living in peace any more. Then on June 19, they killed two of our friends who were Catholic catechists. They killed Frocindo Alvarez right by the church. We heard the shooting.

We left the village to save our lives, and we lost everything in the conflict—our homes, our corn, our beans, our cattle and other animals. Everything is there in Jesús Carranza. So, what are we going to do? We can't go back to get our belongings because the former bar owners have blocked all the entrances. They're the ones responsible for our losses. They're the ones who killed our friends.

When we left, we went to Unión Juárez where the kind people of that town loaned us a piece of land to live on. Now we're trying to start our own community—a new town called San Marcos Antes de la Luz. We've built about one hundred houses, and we're moving people to live there. We're asking the government for credit so we can buy land. We also requested dialogue and negotiations with the Paz y Justicia people. On April 14 of this year (1997), state government representatives did come to Sabanilla to begin negotiations, but it didn't work out. The government offered to help us with housing, food and cooking utensils, but we haven't gotten anything yet. Our situation continues to be desperate, and we're waiting for the materials the government offered so we can finish building our homes.

Then, at the same time as we were trying to negotiate with the government, another friend, Rosey Pérez, was arrested by the Security Police. He's in jail now in Cerro Hueco State Prison. So it doesn't seem like the government is serious about helping us. Our lawyers have proven that the accusations against Rosey are false. He hasn't committed any crimes and it is unjust for him to be in jail still.

Our first demand is freedom for our prisoners. We also need our land back because we are *campesinos* and we need to plant our fields to live. We would like to return to our community, but we need to have a guarantee from the government that it's safe for us to do so. If we can't return to our land, then we need help to build our new community. And we want restitution for what was stolen from us. This is the information that I can give you about our situation as displaced people. Thank you.

### The Jesús Carranza Story (continued)[12]

My name is Marcela Jiménez, and I'm one of the people who were displaced from the town of Jesús Carranza.

A few years ago, my husband, Micario Pérez, was the councilman for the town government. A group of women came to ask him to file a complaint against the bar owners. They wanted to have the illegal bars closed. They said, "We can't stand it anymore. We have no clothes for our poor children. Our husbands spend all their money drinking, and then they beat us."

We filled out a complaint and went to Sabanilla to talk with the mayor. He didn't listen to us. Instead, he put my husband in jail because the four bar owners said he was bothering them. But the women kept organizing to put the bars out of business. After so many complaints, an investigation was started and we presented a formal request to close the bars. I took six of my friends who had injuries from being beaten by their husbands. I said to the mayor, "These are my friends who are suffering because of the bars. But these men don't want to listen to our demands. They only threaten us, and they want to kill my husband. Why? Because he's demanding that they close the bars. And you, Mayor, you put my husband in jail because the bartenders asked you to. Do you listen to them more than to us?"

That was the end of the illegal bars. Everybody, including the bar owners, had to sign an agreement to close them. And my husband got out of jail because they couldn't prove anything against him. That's why they've hated us ever since then. They threaten us. They want to kill us. They want to kill me because I organized the women.

The bar owners are still in Jesús Carranza. They are the leaders of Paz y Justicia. Yes, the same ones. They're rich people—ranchers.

---

[12]From interviews with Marcela Jiménez, Tuxtla Gutiérrez, May 1997.

They got rich dealing alcohol, too. Now they're even richer, because they stole everything from us when we were forced out of the town. They took our cattle, and they sold it.

### The Jesús Carranza Story (continued):[13]

A WOMAN SPEAKS: We are refugees from the town of Jesús Carranza. We left our town on that terrible day of June 19, 1996, when the armed people of Paz y Justicia ran us out. We only had enough time to get our children. We left with nothing. And they killed two of our friends! When the people from Paz y Justicia went trigger-happy, we didn't know where to go or how to get out of there. We ran to the mountains. We fled into the forest. We finally went to live in Unión Juárez where we are now. We don't live in our town anymore.

We had been careful. After the bars closed, we stayed away from the Paz y Justicia people for three months. They were always shooting bullets all over the community. By June 19, they had gotten more weapons. We were happy in our homes that day, working and cooking. I was cooking my tortillas on the fire when those people came with their guns. I was forced out of my home, and I fled, doing the best I could on the spur of the moment. They burned the houses—everything. They sold the cattle and the pigs. They ate the meat.

We heard all the shooting when they attacked the town, but we couldn't defend ourselves. Several of the women ran out under the bullets—women with children, with babies. We almost couldn't get out. We ran as well as we could, with nothing. They destroyed our homes and all our belongings. They finished off everything— our animals, our furniture, everything inside our houses. Thank God all my children got out. Thank God my family is safe.

We were attacked because we are struggling for democracy. We weren't bothering them. We are all *campesinos*. We've had these problems for three years now. They were causing more and more problems, and then they armed themselves.

My son, Rosey Pérez, was unjustly jailed at the *Cerro Hueco*

---

[13]Interview, May 1997.

State Prison here in Tuxtla Gutiérrez. He's been in jail for a year, since July 24 [1996]. He's accused of homicide, but that's a lie. He was coming from the town of Tapijulapa in the state of Tabasco where he went to see his wife. First he went to Tila to get his teacher's papers, because he's a teacher. But the violence had already begun, and the war was going on, and so the police arrested him. They accused him of killing our neighbors. But that's not true, because as I told you, Paz y Justicia did the killings.[14]

And now here we are protesting the government's actions, waiting to see what response the governor will give us. We want a solution. We want to return to our community. When there is an investigation, my friends and I will testify about what really happened—how they ran us out, how they burned our homes, how they shot at us, injured us and killed two of our neighbors. Because we saw it. We lived through it. And we're not afraid any more.

### Return to the North

On July 23 at dawn, the Security Police showed up at the doors of the government building to "invite" the protesters to pick up their things and leave. These were the words of a spokesperson for the displaced in their last press conference in Tuxtla Gutiérrez:

> Between June 15, 1996 and now, 28 of our friends have been killed or disappeared in the municipalities of Tila, Sabanilla, Tumbala and Salto de Agua. Thirty-two are still in jail, and more than 600 arrest warrants are still pending. In addition, 1,150 homes and churches have been destroyed, 3,458 heads of cattle have been stolen and 24 communities are still suffering under Paz y Justicia blockades.
>
> We are leaving, not because we are tired, but because we need to continue our struggle in other ways, always in a peaceful manner. We will never give up, and we hold Gov-

---

[14]Rosey Pérez was freed at the end of the summer of 1997. All charges against him were dropped for lack of evidence.

ernor Julio César Ruíz Ferro[15] responsible if there are any attacks or actions against us or our communities.

All of us are civilian Zapatistas, because the Zapatista ideals of freedom, justice, and dignity are also our ideals. Along with many other Mexicans, we will continue building the country and the world that we all want.[16]

So after 87 days of protest, hundreds of displaced people went back to northern Chiapas with only a partial solution to their demands. Some were able to go back to their communities, but many had to go to refugee settlements. The state government promised to give construction materials to rebuild the homes that had been destroyed by Paz y Justicia. They also promised a few chicken farms as compensation for the more than 3,500 heads of cattle stolen until that date. In exchange for negotiating the freedom of the more than 50 political prisoners, the authorities demanded that the displaced people sign a "non-aggression" pact and begin to dialogue with Paz y Justicia.[17]

### *Northern Chiapas Today[18]*

Today, three years after my conversations with the displaced, the situation in northern Chiapas is still very tense. Paz y Justicia never agreed to have a serious dialogue with the displaced, nor did the government help the victims with any significant reparations for their losses. Although several families returned to their communities, many are still displaced.

In July 2000, I had the opportunity to talk again with some of the people I interviewed for this chapter in 1997. They told me that many communities in Tila and Sabanilla continue to experience serious harassment. People are still unable to travel freely to and from

---

[15]Julio César Ruíz Ferro is also accused of criminal negligence in the 1997 massacre at Acteal. He has not stood trial and is currently the agricultural attaché for the Mexican embassy in Washington, DC.

[16]Quote from *La Jornada,* July 23, 1997.

[17]Angeles Mariscal, *La Jornada*, July 23, 1997.

[18]For more on the displaced of northern Chiapas, consult www.ciepac.org.

their villages because of Paz y Justicia roadblocks. In Masolha Shukha, people had returned to their community, but they are still living in a very tense situation. The villagers told me that they hear shooting every other day, and that they are afraid to go out of the village for fear of harassment from Paz y Justicia. Guadalupe's family never recovered their stolen vehicles. Guadalupe never recovered the body of her murdered son, and justice was never done for his murder. In fact, there has been no justice for any of the families of Masolha Shukha. Several families from Masolha Grande are still displaced today. Some are living in the state of Campeche, some are in San Cristóbal and there are four families from Masolha Grande who are currently living as internal refugees in the village of Masolha Shukha just a few miles away from their own village. These four families have not been able to return to their own community. They have not been able to recover their homes, their land, their livestock or their belongings.

Other people I talked with, like Gloria from Masolha Grande and Margarita from El Limar, continue their activism. Gloria works with displaced people and Margarita continues working as a catequist. Their strength and vitality is contagious, although they still work under difficult conditions and constant harassment. Fear and impunity continue to be part of the scenario in northern Chiapas, as activists are intimidated and threatened. One northern Chiapas activist, José Tila, was assassinated in 1998 when he was on his way to make a statement to United Nations representatives.

By the end of 1997, the low intensity war that had started in these municipalities of northern Chiapas had extended to the highlands—Chenalho' in particular—and later on to *Las Cañadas* and the jungle. In addition to Paz y Justicia, groups like Máscara Roja, the Indigenous Anti-Zapatista Movement (MIRA) and other paramilitary groups began to appear in various parts of the country. By mid-1998, although some of the prisoners from northern Chiapas had been freed, there were hundreds of Zapatista political prisoners from all over Mexico in the Cerro Hueco jail.

The dirty war against the opposition communities in northern Chiapas and other parts of Mexico continues even now after the historic election of opposition candidates to both the presidency of Mexico and the governorship of Chiapas. As these political transitions take place, the situation of low intensity war in northern Chiapas will be a challenge not only for the new governments, but also for Mexican civil society and the international community.

✺

# FIVE

# LAS ABEJAS DE CHENALHO'
# THE COST OF CHOOSING PEACE

# THE PARAMILITARY WAR MOVES TO THE HIGHLANDS

The low intensity war started in northern Chiapas, where the PRI-aligned paramilitary groups such as *Paz y Justicia* and the *"chinchulines"*[1] attacked and killed independent *campesinos* or Zapatista civilian supporters, destroying entire villages and causing thousands of people to abandon their homes and fields. But by summer 1997, the war had moved south to the highlands of Chenalho'.

The story of Chenalho' is another clear illustration of the strategy of low-intensity conflict, where a slow but violent war of attrition is waged against civilians. Among the story's many actors are a group of people called *Las Abejas*—indigenous *campesinos* who have tried to maintain a commitment to active non-violence within a position that is generally supportive of Zapatista ideals.

*Las Abejas,* which means "the bees," were organized in 1993 as a pacifist group related to the Catholic Church in the villages of Los Chorros and Colonia Puebla in the highlands of Chiapas. Paramilitary groups first attacked civilian Zapatista communities and then went after groups like *Las Abejas.* After standing up to the PRI and refusing to participate in armed anti-Zapatista defense patrols, thousands of *Abejas* were run out of their villages in September 1997. They took refuge in San Cristóbal de las Casas, in Zapatista autonomous towns like Polho' and in other nearby towns like Acteal.

Between September and December 1997, communities in the highlands continued to suffer systematic attacks and violence against them. In addition to forcing people from their homes, the paramilitary groups also murdered people in at least 24 communities.[2] Scores of denunciations fell on deaf or complicit ears, and the violence cul-

---

[1] *Paz y Justicia* is the paramilitary group that has been active in Tila and Sabanilla. The *chinchulines* are another group that has operated in Chilón and Bachajón.

[2] According to Bishop Samuel Ruíz, one to nine people were murdered by paramilitary groups in each of 24 different highland communities between September and December 1997.

170 Never Again A World Without Us

minated in the tragic massacre of 45 children, women and men in Acteal in December 1997.

### San Pedro Chenalho'

San Pedro Chenalho' is located in the highlands of Chiapas, about 70 kilometers from San Cristóbal. According to a December 1994 census, there are 30,680 inhabitants in the municipality of Chenalho', the majority of whom are Mayan Tzotzil. Ninety percent of the Chenalho' population lives in homes with dirt-floors, 88 percent of homes have no indoor plumbing, and 51 percent of people under 15 years old are illiterate.[3]

The main economic activities in Chenalho' are agriculture and forestry. Coffee production plays an especially important role. High quality organic Chenalho' coffee is produced by small farmers organized into the unions and cooperatives of COPCAFE and is exported to the United States and Europe through fair trade initiatives.[4] Over two-thirds of the land in Chenalho' is collectively owned by indigenous people, either as communal land or as *ejidos*.[5]

The political situation in Chenalho' is very unstable and complex. The government has always been in the hands of the PRI—a political party characterized by corruption, authoritarianism and electoral fraud. The two primary opposition parties in Chenalho' are the Democratic Revolution Party (PRD) and the Cardenista Front for National Reconstruction.[6] In 1997, however, the Cardenista Front joined forces with the PRI in the paramilitary war against civilian Zapatistas and independent groups like *Las Abejas*.

---

[3]*The Road to the Massacre: Special Report on Chenalho'*, Fray Bartolomé de las Casas Human Rights Center, December 1997. pp. 1-6.

[4]Fair trade is a movement in which organizations in developed countries work together with agricultural cooperatives of small coffee producers to help the farmers sell their coffee at a guaranteed and fair price. Today, there is an international network of "fair traders" in Europe, the United States and Canada that both sells coffee and educates people about the ways in which the globalized economy is hurting small farmers.

[5]*The Road to the Massacre*, p. 6.

[6]See chapter 4, p. 136 for a brief background on the Cardenista Front.

# CHENALHO'

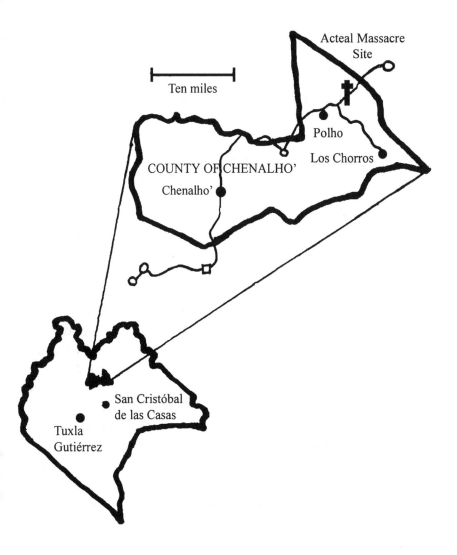

The Zapatista movement in Chenalho' has grown tremendously since 1994, becoming the most important and active opposition to the official government. This growth has been manifested in the formation of civilian Zapatista bases of support. Because civilian Zapatistas want to be governed by an autonomous system, and because the Zapatista movement believes in democracy from the bottom up, many Zapatista civilians do not participate in elections.[7] In 1995, a Zapatista autonomous government was created in the town of Pohlo', with its own authorities and officers. As is the case in all autonomous regions, the Autonomous Council of Polho' does not accept any type of government aid or interference.[8]

Chenalho' is a strategic region for both Zapatistas and the Mexican Army. It is a crossroads between the highlands, the northern zone and the rainforest. The town of Polho', where the Autonomous Council of Polho' resides, is a geographical and strategic center for the Zapatistas, because of direct access to paths from the jungle into the highland *aguascalientes* of Oventik. For this reason, Polho' became a logical target for the Army in the counterinsurgency war against the EZLN. In order to cut off access and destroy the Zapatista base of support, the Army directed the war at the civilian population (both Zapatistas and independent groups such as *Las Abejas*) in village after village throughout the entire municipality of Chenalho'.

Human rights organizations charge that the paramilitary groups in Chenalho' were trained and supported by the leaders of *Paz y Justicia*, PRI state representatives, and the Mayor of Chenalho', as well as the Mexican security forces, including the Mexican Federal Army.

Interviews in this chapter took place after the initial displacement of *Las Abejas* from their towns, both immediately before and after the Acteal massacre. Due to the emergency situation in which these interviews were conducted, they were done with the spokespeople available—in this case, men rather than women.

---

[7] Under some conditions, some Zapatista civilians do vote—especially for opposition parties like the PRD.
[8] *The Road to the Massacre*, pp. 1-6.

# LAS ABEJAS DE CHENALHO'

## *1. CATHOLICS, ACTIVISTS, REFUGEES: INTERVIEWS WITH ALONSO*

*In September 1997, a group of men and women from the municipality of Chenalho' arrived as refugees to San Cristóbal de las Casas. Their villages—Los Chorros and Colonia Puebla—had been attacked, and armed civilian members of the PRI had burned down their homes. Many of them were small coffee producers—members of organic coffee cooperatives that export through fair-trade. Their attackers had taken their land and picked their coffee, selling it on the black market in order to get money to buy more weapons.*

*The refugees who were members of Las Abejas de Chenalho' found shelter at a school-convent in San Cristóbal. I met them in San Cristóbal a couple of weeks after their arrival, when four of them were hired for day-work in carpentry at an artisan project run by our organization. It was then that I learned about their plight. From September to December, I conducted a series of interviews with Alonso López Méndez, one of the Chenalho' refugees. He told me about how* Las Abejas *were formed, about his work with the Church and about the beginnings of the conflict that had forced his community to become refugees.*

### *"Why are they Attacking Us?"*[9]

Why are they attacking us? I don't know. I don't know why there is this problem. We didn't cause this problem. We stay in our houses, eating when we can. When we cannot, we have to see how to find a little food. We work so that we eat. We work in the cornfield. We work with the coffee. We work together in the coffee cooperative. Those of us who have no land go to the plantations far away to find our work. Some of these towns in Chenalho' used to be plantations, but the workers took over the land a long time ago, and now

---

[9]From a series of interviews with Alonso López Méndez, September to December, 1997.

they are *ejidos*. As *campesinos*, we organized to take the land and form *ejidos*. We organized together back then. So, why is it that we are fighting now? In Chenalho' we don't even have problems with religion like other people do. We have never been like in other places, like in Chamula where the Catholics expelled the evangelicals. They're always fighting over religion. But we don't. Here, we have no differences. Presbyterians and Catholics work together translating the Bible. So, we can't understand why there is this violence now. Why are they suddenly attacking us? We don't understand it. Where are the weapons coming from? Who is arming our neighbors? Who is telling them that we are the enemy just because we don't want to be with the PRI, just because we don't want to kill the Zapatistas who are our brothers and sisters? Why?

### Las Abejas

We are part of the civil society of Chenalho', which means that we are civilians. We are peaceful people. We don't carry weapons. We are religious people. We are organized to defend our rights and to search for peaceful solutions to the conflict. We don't belong to any political party. We have the same demands as the Zapatistas. We believe in the same things they believe in. We want change just like they do. We want justice and freedom and democracy just like they do. But we don't carry weapons, not even to defend ourselves.

We are called *Las Abejas* because we are like the "bees." We have stingers. Do you know what we do with our stingers? We sting. We will sting the government until we get what we're struggling for— until we achieve peace and justice, freedom and democracy. We are very organized just like the bees are. You know the bees have a queen? We have a queen too. Our queen is our organization. We protect our queen, and we take care of her. We are all workers in our organization. We are all united, and we work together for the good of our queen. Nobody is better than anyone else, and we all work hard. You know the bees have these little antennas up here on their forehead? Well, we have antennas also. We use them to communicate with one another, to help one another, to know what is happening to our brothers and sisters when they need help. We use our antennas to be united and organized. We use our antennas to know what is happening around us, so that we are prepared. The bees fly from flower to flower. We also move fast from town to town throughout Chenalho'.

We organized as *Las Abejas* in 1993. At that time, five of our catechists had been falsely accused of murder and taken to jail. What happened was that two families were fighting over a piece of land. They fought, and some people came to attack the others. The women were raped, a man was killed and two other men were injured. The PRI authorities falsely accused our five catechist friends of this crime, and they were arrested and taken to jail even though other people had committed the crime. It was an injustice. They accused them because they didn't like us, because we always spoke up against the wrong-doing we saw. In that case our friends defended the victims, particularly the women. The PRI authorities never liked that. So, they accused them.

We investigated with the help of our lawyers and we found out that our friends were innocent. So all of us members of the Catholic Church in Chenalho' organized to have demonstrations, meetings, sit-ins and—since we're Christian—lots of prayer. Finally, we were successful, and our friends were freed. At that time, we organized the group *Las Abejas* because we saw we were successful if we worked together.

First, *Las Abejas* was an organization of Catholic catechists and lay people, but in 1994 it changed and became more open. After the Zapatista uprising, we formed an organization called "The Chenalho *Las Abejas* Civil Society" in order to work for peace in Chiapas. In the organization *Las Abejas* there are now Catholics, evangelicals, Presbyterians and *costumbristas*—who are the people that practice the old Mayan religion. There are about 3,000 of us adult *Abejas* in 24 communities of Chenalho'. If there is a meeting we all go together, united.

As members of civil society and as people who want peace, we go to the peace marches, and we participated in the "peace belts" around the place where the San Andrés Peace Talks were held.[10] Our goal is to struggle for a peaceful solution to the war. Our work as *Abejas* is to analyze our situation—to think about how we live and what the government is doing to us. We reflect on these things through the Word of God. We think, "What did Jesus do when he suffered troubles as we suffer now? What road did he take?" We think, "It's true that we are poor, but we know that Jesus walked among the poor." We trust in God. We know that before the year 2000 there will be a change in the world, peace in the world, democracy in the world. These are our goals as members of *Las Abejas*.

### *The Tzotzil Bible of Chenalho': An Ecumenical Project*

The translation of the Bible is an example of the way we can work together. This is an ecumenical project between Presbyterians and Catholics. I am a catechist, a coordinator of catechists, and a Tzotzil-Spanish and Tzeltal-Spanish translator. When I finished elementary school, I couldn't read or write in my own language—only in Spanish. Then the priests helped me. They said, "You will learn to write in Tzotzil." I learned to type, and I learned to use the computer. I started working with the team of Bible translators with Father Alberto from Canada, and with brother René and his wife Carla, who are Presbyterian. These people are intelligent. They speak the Mayan languages. They are good people. We worked together in this team of Catholics and Presbyterians to translate the Bible into Tzotzil. We call it *The Chenalho' Bible*, and we've worked together on it with no problems.

In the old days we used to fight over religion. Not seriously—not like in Chamula. We only had problems with the evangelicals because they didn't want to chip in for the patron saint feast days, and as Catholics, we always gave money. We made fun of each other.

---

[10]When representatives of the EZLN met with representatives of the Mexican Federal Government to negotiate and sign the first peace accords in San Andrés, "peace belts"—or human chains—were formed around the buildings where the negotiations were held in order to protect the negotiators. The peace belt at San Andrés had three rings, one made up of members of the Mexican security forces, one of Red Cross volunteers and one of concerned Mexican citizens.

The evangelicals would say, "Those Catholics spend all their money and time drinking alcohol. They have parties, and they worship idols." Because they call the images of the saints in the church "idols." We also made fun of them and called them names. We didn't fight like in other places where they kill each other. We just fought a little. But that was before. Then God won our hearts. But now, it seems that they are being lost again.

René, a Presbyterian brother, and his wife Carla are good friends of Tatik Samuel[11] and they had a nice talk with him. They made an agreement to produce *The Chenalho' Bible* together as Catholics and Presbyterians. Father Alberto requested two computers from the National Bible Society in Mexico—one for the Presbyterians and one for us Catholics. We started to work, and people from both religions came from many communities to work on this. We translated, and they translated. We corrected their work, and they corrected ours. That's why there are no mistakes in our Bible. We worked on the Bible translation for about five or six years with the Presbyterian brothers and sisters of Chenalho'. Now we have finished our work.

Many years ago, the Presbyterians translated the old Tzotzil Bible all by themselves. This is the Bible we always had before. But the translation of the old Tzotzil Bible is wrong.[12] Those translators had bad ideas, ideas that are not from the Mayans. They are foreign ideas. We Catholics of Chenalho' follow Indian theology, and we speak the way our Mayan ancestors spoke. We introduced these old Mayan words and thoughts into the new Bible. For example, there's a word in the Bible that means "healers," and in the old Bible they translated it as "witch doctors." That shows no respect for the Bible. We respect what it says in the Bible. Brother René and Father Alberto know the ancient Bible, and they understand the Greek language and the Hebrew language. The old Bible is written in these languages. So if we don't know what a word means in Spanish, we will see the mean-

---

[11]Tatik Samuel is the name the Mayans have given Bishop Samuel Ruíz. Tatik is an indigenous word meaning father.
[12]The Tzotzil Bible used in Chenalho' before 1997 was translated by the conservative Wycliff Bible Society.

ing in Hebrew or Greek, and we will use the same word in Tzotzil. We know that an *ilol* in Tzotzil is not a "witch doctor," he is a "healer." And the sun is not *kakal* or "day," like they translated before. The "sun" is *tatik,* our father. The sun is our father and the moon is our mother, *metik.* Everybody knows that. We argued about this a lot, but in the end, that's what we wrote in our Bible.

We already finished the work of translation and we're just waiting for the big celebration in February when we will receive our copies of the Bibles.

The problem now is that we have all these conflicts in Chenalho'. Since September we've been at war. On October 4 there was a big march of civil society groups and *Las Abejas* participated. The march was against the war. It was against the conflicts we are suffering in our communities, because people who are from the PRI are attacking Zapatistas and *Abejas* and burning our houses, and so many of us have had to flee our communities. At the demonstration we said we wanted no more troubles, no more war and no more killing one another. The march started in San Cristóbal de las Casas and finished in the municipal seat, San Pedro de Chenalho'. A Catholic brother named José spoke at the rally. He spoke well, with the truth. He said, "We can't be killing each other now, and then acting as if nothing had happened when we have our fiestas. We must always treat each other like brothers and sisters in Christ."

### The Conflict over the Majomut Sand-Pit

The conflict started in Los Chorros, which is my community. It was over a sand-pit. It started in September of this year, 1997. Before that, there had been problems in another *ejido* called Colonia Puebla, over a road. That was in May.

The majority of communities in Chenalho' are hamlets—very old hamlets with communal land. Now there are also the autonomous communities, part of the Autonomous Council in Polho' that formed early this year. They are Zapatistas, the bases of support for the EZLN. The autonomous communities are also hamlets, but now they have declared themselves autonomous from the government.

Then, there are the *ejidos*. These are new communities. A long time ago, they used to be plantations. The workers took the land, and everybody was supposed to get a parcel from the government and become *ejidos*. Los Chorros, Puebla, Yashemel and Yibeljo are *ejidos*. Except we still haven't got the papers. Maybe we never will get the papers. It doesn't matter now. Now all we want is to be able to return to our towns, to our land, to our homes. My community is an *ejido* that used to be a plantation. It is called Ejido Los Chorros and it's the biggest *ejido* en Chenalho'. About 400 families are owners of the *ejido*, and about 600 more are not; we are landless. Now everybody calls Los Chorros a paramilitary town, because the PRI guards have taken it over. But that's not the way it was before. Before it was a peaceful town.

There's a parcel of land close to Los Chorros called Majomut that has a sand-pit on it. The people of Los Chorros say that Majomut belongs to Los Chorros. The Zapatistas say it belongs to the Autonomous Council of Polho', because it's inside Polho's town limits. After the armed conflict began in 1994, many *campesinos* started to take land. This happened in Chenalho' as well. A group of landless men took over the Majomut parcel. They are members of the Cardenista Front, but when they took the land they pretended to be Zapatistas.[13] They wore ski masks and they put up a sign that said EZLN. The next day they said, "No, we are Cardenistas," and they put up a new sign. They took over and started to charge 20 pesos for a truckload of sand. They just wanted to make a business out of this, and take advantage of all of us.[14]

The Zapatistas got mad, because this parcel is next to Polho', and because the Cardenistas were charging for the sand. The Zapatistas said, "Why did these people take our land pretending to be Zapatistas

---

[13]For more information on the sand-pit conflict, see *The Road to the Massacre: Special Report on Chenalho'*, Fray Bartolomé de las Casas Human Rights Center, December 1997, pp. 8-10, 17, 18.

[14]Sand is used for making the concrete blocks that some houses are made of. It is also an important material for the construction of roads. Although the government provides some resources for road construction, communities often provide labor and some of the materials. Access to sand can speed up a community's chances of getting a road.

when they are not? Why are they selling the sand to indigenous people when we are all indigenous? The sand-pit is part of Polho' and that land is automonous. We're going to take back this sand-pit so that the people of Chenalho' won't have to pay for getting sand." The Zapatistas said it was their land because in April 1997 they declared themselves autonomous, and Majomut was part of their territory. So in August 1997 the Zapatistas took the sand-pit back from the Cardenistas, and they started to give away the sand to whoever needed it. You just had to let them know you needed it and it was free.

The Cardenistas tried to find a way to get back the sand-pit and to get revenge. They made an agreement with the PRI people to fight the Zapatistas. The PRI and Cardenistas used to be enemies. In 1979, when the Cardenista Front was called the Socialist Workers Party, the PRI people hated them, because they were the opposition. In 1979 they had a conflict, and the PRI authorities tortured some of the Cardenistas. But now they are friends, and they're allied against the Zapatistas. It's a very complicated war.

In July there was an assembly in Los Chorros. A teacher from Yabteclum—a PRI member—had been killed, and the PRI people were accusing the Zapatistas of the murder. The Zapatistas said that the PRI people had killed the teacher for speaking up against the violence. It's true. In an assembly one day, he said he was against the violence, and next day he was found dead. The Zapatistas also accused PRI members of kidnapping two fellow Zapatistas.

Then, a Cardenista leader came to Los Chorros offering a box of refreshments and asking for support from the PRI authorities and from the townspeople to fight the Zapatistas. The *Ejido* Commissioner who was a member of the PRI said, "We are *ejido* owners. We aren't illegal Zapatistas like them. We can take the land from them, sell the sand, and make lots of money from it. We'll buy weapons, make defense patrols, get training, and then attack them. We'll show those Zapatistas that we have power." That's how the Cardenistas and the PRI people made their agreement.

All the PRI people agreed with this and talked about how to get the weapons, where to get money and who could help them. At that time there weren't that many PRI people in Los Chorros. Later on the

PRI took over the town. They started to recruit people for their guards. Everybody had to serve in the defense patrols, even if they didn't want to. The *Abejas* were not in agreement with this. We said that we should talk with the Zapatistas about how to share the sand-pit, that we should have a dialogue. We said that we had to analyze the situation first and look for a peaceful way to solve the problem. When we said this, they accused us of being Zapatistas. They said, "If you love the Zapatistas so much, it's because you're Zapatistas yourselves!" Every week there was a meeting like this. The majority of people agreed with us. But the PRI and Cardenistas had more power. They bought weapons and called the PRI people in Colonia Puebla to supply them with more. They bought high caliber weapons like AK-47s. We're not sure where they get their weapons, but we've heard that they buy them in San Cristóbal. The PRI people from Colonia Puebla know where to get arms. They also knew where to get the money and the training to use the weapons. They say the Mayor of Chenalho' also helps them. Jacinto Arias Cruz is the mayor of Chenalho'. He's the "official" Municipal President. He's from the PRI, but he's associated now with the Cardenista Front.[15]

When we refused to participate in the defense patrols, they demanded that we pay money. First we had to pay 100 pesos, then it was 500 pesos. They did this in Los Chorros, but before Los Chorros it was in Colonia Puebla, then in Yashemel, then in other hamlets and *ejidos*. All over Chenalho', the PRI people organized in this way, as "defense patrols." In Colonia Puebla they tortured four *Abejas* men because they refused to participate in the defense patrols. They put them in jail and beat them up for refusing to participate and for refusing to pay money. One of these men was a very old man, the father of my friend Tomás.

There are Zapatista supporters in my community and in other

---

[15]This conversation took place in October 1997 when Jacinto Arias was still the mayor of Chenalho'. He is currently serving a jail term for aiding in the transportation of firearms to the site of the Acteal massacre. He is also accused of providing money for the arms and ammunition.

autonomous towns. The paramilitary guards attacked them first, shooting at them, trying to push them out of the villages. They also burned their houses. Finally, the Zapatistas fled. The Zapatistas all went to Polho' or to Narajatic Alto or to other places that are autonomous regions. They say that hundreds, maybe thousands, of Zapatistas fled to the mountains.

Then they came after us—*Las Abejas*—because we refused to participate in the patrols. They started shooting at our houses. They threatened to kill us. They started the shooting on August 30, and it went on every night around midnight, until September 15. They said they were going to kill us on September 15, because it was Independence Day—a holiday—and nobody would pay attention. I stayed inside my house and didn't go out anymore after I heard that. Finally on Sepember 15, I left my community with several other men. We left our wives back there and came to San Cristóbal. Since that day we've been refugees here along with a couple hundred other people. Thousands of Zapatistas and *Abejas* have also fled to the mountains of Chenalho' or to Polho'.[16]

Many of us left our wives that day in our communities of Los Chorros and Colonia Puebla. When the PRI guards saw that we weren't there, they threatened our wives. They said they would kill them if they didn't pay 10,000 pesos. What could my wife do? She didn't have any money, so she sold all our corn and our coffee plants. I used to have 3,000 coffee plants—good coffee, organic coffee for export. Now I have nothing. Nothing! That's what happened to all of us and to the Zapatistas. We all had very good coffee that we used to sell to the cooperative. The PRI guards stole the coffee when we fled. They harvested it all to sell to the illegal buyers. They bought more

---

[16]After the Acteal massacre on December 22, 1997, there were more than 8,000 internal refugees from many communities of Chenalho' in the nine camps of Pohlo'. They had all fled the paramilitary violence in their communities and found refuge in Zapatista autonomous territory. In 1999, the number was over 10,000 according to statistics from independent human rights sources.

arms and more ammunition with the money.[17]

On September 18 they started to burn the *Abejas'* houses, just like they burned the Zapatista's houses before. They didn't burn my house because my wife was still there. But she couldn't leave the house because she was too afraid of getting killed. Before they burned the houses they stole everything inside. They stole TVs, radios, furniture, clothes, pots and pans, food, corn, coffee, pigs, chickens, everything. Everything! They sold it very cheap in other towns and they bought more weapons with their money. Whatever they couldn't steal they set on fire. They burned hundreds of houses in our communities—Zapatista houses, *Abeja* houses. Some people had good block and cement houses that "Habitat" helped them build.[18] They couldn't burn those houses so they used hammers to destroy them. Now there are only walls full of big holes. Then, the PRI people went to Polho' to attack the Zapatistas. They attacked, but the Zapatistas defended themselves, and the PRI people ran all the way back to Los Chorros.

### A Crime Foretold

*My last interview with Alonso was on December 21,1997, what turned out to be just one day before the Acteal massacre. On that day, he was still a refugee in San Cristóbal, and his unease was grow-*

---

[17]In Chenalho', small coffee growers are organized into coffee cooperatives and unions who export the high quality organic coffee through the fair trade network. The cooperatives and union in Chenalho' suffered serious economic losses from the low intensity war. From September to December 1997, precisely at harvest time, paramilitary groups evicted hundreds of coffee producers from their land, robbed them of their crop and sold the coffee on the black market. In 1998 the Zapatista and *Abejas* producers were able to go back to their fields to harvest their coffee with the help of human rights accompaniers. Today (2000), the coffee is again being sold to the cooperatives and much of the economic infrastructure is being re-established.

[18]Habitat for Humanity is a non-profit organization that helps provide housing in areas of need. It has a community-based cooperative project in the highlands of Chiapas that involves the local people in the decision-making and in the construction of their own homes. When the counter-insurgency war hit Chenalho' in September 1997, paramilitary groups destroyed hundreds of the houses built through this project. The houses destroyed were those of Zapatista or *Abejas* families.

*ing daily as threats increased. His words are chilling to me now, because of the nature of the brutality that followed and the unwillingness of government and security forces to prevent this tragedy.*

### "We've Asked the Police for Help, But They Won't Help Us!"

Some defense patrol people from Los Chorros have come to San Cristóbal to buy weapons and to look for us. They've sworn that if they find us, they'll throw gasoline on us and burn us alive. We have to be very careful not to go out in the streets of San Cristóbal. Have you seen them? They come in their pickup trucks with the security police behind them. They drive all over the hamlets of Chenalho' in their pickup trucks, and the security police protect them. We've asked for help from the police, but they won't help us. We've talked to the municipal authorities with no result. We went to Tuxtla to talk with the state authorities, but it was to no avail. The Governor says on TV that there are no paramilitary groups. He also says there are no displaced people from Chenalho'. What are we then?

What are we going to do? My poor wife is suffering all alone. She can't get out, and I can't go back to my town. Hundreds of people—thousands of people—are in the mountains, in the forest. They are cold and they don't have food. What are we going to do? We don't know. We are looking for ways to return. The Zapatistas are helping people when they come into Polho' even if they are not Zapatistas. But they're suffering, too, and there's not enough food for so many homeless people.

We are very concerned, very worried. Just a short time ago the PRI guards from Los Chorros went to La Esperanza again to burn houses. Then they burned the houses of the Zapatistas in Acteal. There are many refugees hiding in Acteal—both *Abejas* and Zapatistas. The paramilitary people have sworn that they'll go there and kill them all. They have sworn they'll attack the Zapatistas at Polho'. They say they'll burn us alive if they find us. We are extremely worried.

### 2. THE ACTEAL MASSACRE: JOSE'S STORY

*On December 22, 1997, sixty heavily armed men dressed in black fatigues opened fire on and killed forty-five unarmed Tzotzil men, women and children in Acteal. When the massacre began, the victims had been praying and fasting for peace in a small chapel in a makeshift refugee settlement hidden deep in the forest of Chenalho', in the highlands of Chiapas. Like Alonso, they were* Abejas, *poor campesinos known for their dedication to hard work, their commitment to peace and reconciliation and their deep faith. They had been violently evicted from their communities for refusing to participate in paramilitary activity against civilian Zapatistas.*

*Three days after the massacre, I went to Acteal for the funeral service. José, a catechist from* Las Abejas, *gave us the following account of what he had seen when he arrived in Acteal with the Red Cross the morning after the massacre.*

## "We Asked for Help. They Did Nothing."[19]

Three days ago, on December 22, paramilitary patrols attacked. These assassins are from Los Chorros and from other communities that they control now. They are members of the PRI party. They organized themselves into paramilitary groups in order to attack the Zapatista civilian supporters and to attack those of us who are members of civil society. They've been carrying out these attacks for a long time, ever since May when they started organizing in Colonia Puebla, Los Chorros and other villages.

First they went after the Zapatista supporters—the ones who are struggling for autonomy. There are Zapatista civilians in almost every hamlet and *ejido* of Chenalho', not just in Polho'. The PRI people decided that they wanted the Zapatistas out. They started all kinds of fights. In Colonia Puebla they started a fight over a road. In Los Chorros they started a fight over a sand-pit. That was in May. Then they formed their paramilitary patrols and bought their weapons, good ones like AK-47s. It seems that the mayor of Chenalho' and other authorities are supporting them.

The PRI patrols burned the Zapatistas' houses and shot at them. Finally, the people fled. They went into the mountains and into other villages. But most of them went to the autonomous town of Polho'.

---

[19]From an interview with José at Acteal, December 25, 1997.

Then the paramilitary patrols started to attack us. We are members of an organization called *Las Abejas*. We are peaceful people, church people. Many of us are catechists. They tried to force us to attack the Zapatistas by making us participate in the patrols. If people didn't want to do this, they would get killed, or they had to pay lots of money, which was used by the paramilitaries to buy more weapons and ammunition. We *Abejas* refused to help, so they came after us too.

It was in September that they started to attack the Zapatistas and us. Since then, thousands of people have had to flee the paramilitary violence. Refugees are hiding in the mountains. Others have set up refugee camps in villages. Many people went to Polho'. There are about 8,000 people in Pohlo' now. In X'oyep, where I live, very close to Pohlo', there are about a thousand people, all *Abejas* and refugees mostly.

Three days ago the massacre happened here in Acteal. The attackers came from Los Chorros, Esperanza, Ximich, K'anjolal, Pechiquil, and Ixtajalucum. They came dressed in dark blue and black—like the security police—and they were wearing black ski masks. They came to attack the Zapatistas, who were camping down the hill. They wanted to attack the people from Quextic, who are Zapatista civilians, who also came here to Acteal to find refuge from the violence. *Las Abejas* were at the chapel praying and fasting for a peaceful solution to the conflict. They had been there for two days already and were about to start their third day of fasting. They were praying for a safe return to their communities. They were praying for peace in Chenalho'.

Zapatistas from other villages who knew there was going to be an attack came to Acteal to warn the people. Some of our *Abejas* friends knew about the attack, too, because they had heard about the big meeting on Sunday night where the PRI people planned it. So our friends came here to Acteal at about midnight to warn people, but they didn't know exactly when the attack was going to happen. Besides, we couldn't defend ourselves anyway. None of us have weapons. We had been telling the authorities all along that we were in danger, but nothing was ever done to help us.

The attackers got to Acteal, and they hid. Then they decided to go into the chapel to look for Zapatista supporters. It was about ten-thirty or eleven in the morning when they started their attack. They attacked when the *Abejas* were praying—shot them in the back as they knelt in the chapel! Some people tried to escape into the woods, but the murderers chased them into the ravines, shooting at them with high caliber weapons and exploding bullets. People were killed right here, and over there. Here is where we found some of the bodies. The shooting went on all day, from eleven in the morning until four in the afternoon.

Two survivors were able to go to San Cristóbal where we were and tell us that people had been killed. We asked the Red Cross to help us, and we got to Acteal about 1:30 in the morning on the 23rd. The first thing we saw was a bunch of dead bodies. The Red Cross said they couldn't get the bodies out yet. They needed to do it right. We had to go all the way to the town of Majomut where the sand-pit is because there's a Security Police checkpoint there. We went there and came back with the police.

We got back to Acteal again at 4:30 in the morning. We found 45 people dead: 21 women, 15 children and 9 men. All of them were *Abejas*. We took the bodies out one by one. I kept looking at the poor people. The women were naked. One woman's head had been shattered with an exploding bullet. A young girl's body had been chopped in half with a machete. Another girl had a broken skull. Little by little we kept getting the bodies out.

We finished recovering the bodies at about 6:15 in the morning. That's when we saw a woman come from the forest holding a child. She wasn't injured, and neither was her child, but she told us how she had laid on the floor of the chapel for hours with all the dead bodies around her. She told us all about the shooting, and how she ran to the forest to hide after the shooting stopped. The poor woman was crying when we found her.

Nineteen other people were injured. They're in hospitals in San Cristóbal and Tuxtla. It's so terrible what happened here! I can't stand it! These people who were killed were not members of my family, but still I care about them because they were members of my organization, *Las Abejas*. I started to cry, to call to them, but they couldn't hear me any more. They were all dead. I saw a little baby boy, his broken body, lying over there. "Poor little angel, what happened to you?" He couldn't answer. It was so hard!

We had been demanding a solution to the conflict for several months! We asked for a dialogue. But the mayor of Chenalho' was opposed to the peace talks. We went all the way to the Public Ministry. We asked for the attacks against us to be investigated. We even gave the names of the perpetrators. They didn't pay any attention to our petition. They did nothing.

We are acting in a peaceful way, and they don't listen to us. They give us no solutions. So, we are thinking of going farther than these actions. Because, what else can we do? The PRI authorities don't want us to be organized. They don't want a road to peace. What they want is for us to fight the Zapatistas. They don't want anyone other than themselves to be in power.

The Zapatistas want democracy and justice. We also want democracy and justice. This is why the paramilitary groups are after us. And actually, not all PRI people agree to this violence. Many of them are against it. But the people in power kill their own people who oppose the violence. One man made very good arguments against using violence, and they burned his house, robbed his coffee harvest and made him leave.

We know who caused this violence. We have their names. But we don't know where they get their weapons. We don't know who gives them orders. We need to find out. We need justice.

## 3. THE FUNERAL MASS IN THE MOUNTAINS[20]

"...cuch'umal ch'ul sinyora stot, sinyora sme', ch'ul banasmil,
ch'ul viajel, mu xa jip xatenuncutic..."

"...one hundred times, holy mother and father, holy mother,
holy earth, holy heaven, do not abandon us..."[21]

The early morning fog was just starting to clear away in the
mountains and ravines of the Chiapas highlands as we walked in
silent procession with hundreds of Indian mourners. We walked up
and down the winding road, behind the trucks that carried the coffins
containing the murdered bodies of 15 children, 21 women and 9 men.
The sad notes of guitars and the high nasal chanting of Mayan voices
accompanied the long, piercing, owl-like beeps of the vehicle horns.
The stench of death permeated the cold mountain air and blended
with the odors of incense, candles and flowers. As Bishop Samuel
Ruíz would later call it, this was "the saddest Christmas of our life-
time."

The procession was interrupted when a truck full of people, followed by a security police vehicle, drove slowly towards the marchers. In the back of the truck a group of men tried to hide behind the
women and children. But they were recognized. They were people
who had taken part in the violence of the December 22 massacre in
Acteal. "Those are the people who murdered our loved ones," people
started to call out. Without violence, the marchers pulled 16 men
down off the truck and escorted them to a police vehicle, which drove
them away. We wondered if these men had been arrested or were
merely being escorted to their safety—if they would be taken to jail
or to a hiding place. Just a few days earlier, we had seen these same
members of paramilitary groups driving through the communities in

---

[20]Excerpts from "The Funeral Mass in the Mountains" by Teresa Ortiz. First
appeared in December 1997 issue of Cloudforest Initiatives newsletter, *Utopías*.
[21]Translated from Tzotzil from *Rites to Ask for Life*, by the Coordinating Team for
Indian Theology, Parish of San Pedro Chenalho', Diocese of San Cristóbal de las
Casas, Chiapas.

similar trucks, insulting and harassing—accompanied then, too, by the security police.

It was about eight o'clock when we arrived in Acteal. We walked down by the open area where Bishop Samuel Ruíz and others were to celebrate the funeral Mass, and farther down the hill to where a dozen men dug long trenches for the graves. Deep in the ravine, we could still see a pile of blood-stained clothes. We could also see the bullet marks on the tree trunks and the "cave" where a teenage boy and his six-year-old brother had hid for several hours as their mother and baby brother were murdered. We stood there watching the men work, weeping in silent rage, as three of our *Abejas* friends came to stand with us. "It is so good that you came," is all they said.

Bishop Samuel Ruíz and three priests presided over a beautiful and emotional outdoor funeral Mass. They stood under a canopy of banana leaves, facing the 15 small white children's coffins, the 30 adult coffins, the relatives and the survivors of the massacre. Hundreds of Mayan-Tzotzil people had come to bid farewell to loved ones with Mayan rituals and rhythmic chanting, with candles and incense and chrysanthemums, with Christian prayers, with testimonies, with tears, sadness and rage. National and international visitors cried angry tears. There were even tears in the eyes of journalists and photographers who had come to cover the event.

A small girl moved about behind the legs of tall photographers trying to get a look at the ceremony. Tatik Samuel was blessing the bodies and talking about justice as the relatives covered the coffins with white and yellow chrysanthemums. The girl finally came and stood next to me, her entire body shaking as she cried silently. I held her tight trying to protect what I could no longer protect.

"...Li oy jch'ix atoj, li' oy jch'ix acantela, yu'un li' tal squelot, li' tal yilot, li cuts' calaltique..."

*"...here are your candles, here is your incense, here I came to see you, I came to visit you, your relative..."*[22]

---

[22]Translated from Tzotzil from *Rite of Death*, by the Coordinating Team for Indian Theology, Parish of San Pedro Chenalho', Diocese of San Cristóbal de las Casas, Chiapas.

# THE VICTIMS[23]

María Pérez Oyalte, Age 42
Martha Capote Pérez, Age 12
Rosa Vázquez Luna, Age 24
Marcela Capote Ruíz, Age 29
Marcela Pucuj Luna, Age 67
Loida Ruíz Gómez, Age 6
Catarina Luna Pérez, Age 21
Manuela Paciencia Moreno, Age 35
Manuel Santiz Culebra, Age 57
Margarita Méndez Paciencia, Age 23
Marcela Luna Ruíz, Age 35
Micaela Vázquez Pérez, Age 9
Josefa Vázquez Pérez, Age 6
Daniel Gómez Pérez, Age 24
Sebastián Gómez Pérez, Age 9
Juana Pérez Pérez, Age 33, (7 months pregnant)
María Gómez Ruíz, Age 23, (7 months pregnant)
Victorio Vázquez Gómez, Age 22
Verónica Vázquez Luna, Age 20
Paulina Hernández Vázquez, Age 22
Juana Pérez Luna, Age 9
Roselia Gómez Hernández, Age 5
Lucia Méndez Capote, Age 7
Graciela Gómez Hernández, Age 3
Marcela Capote Vásquez, Age 15  (pregnant)
Miguel Pérez Jiménez, Age 40
Susana Jiménez Pérez, Age 17
Rosa Pérez Pérez, Age 33 (pregnant)
Ignacio Pucuj Luna, Age 62
María Luna Méndez, Age 44

---

[23]From *Acteal: Entre el duelo y la lucha* (San Cristóbal de las Casas, Chiapas, Mexico: Centro de Derechos Humanos Fray Bartolomé de las Casas, 1998) and *Acteal: Una herida abierta* (Tlaquepaque, Jalisco, Mexico: Instituto Tecnológicio y de Estudios Superiores de Occidente, 1998).

Alonso Vásquez Gómez, Age 46
Lorenzo Gómez Pérez, Age 46
María Capote Pérez, Age 16
Antonia Vázquez Luna, Age 27
Antonia Vázquez Pérez, Age 21
Marcela Vázquez Pérez, Age 30
Silvia Pérez Luna, Age 6
Vicente Méndez Capote, Age 5
Guadalupe Gómez Hernández, Age 2
Margarita Vázquez Luna, Age 3
Juana Vázquez Luna, 8 months old
Alejandro Pérez Luna, Age 16
Juana Luna Vázquez, Age 45
Juana Gómez Pérez, Age 61
Juan Carlos Luna Pérez, Age 2

## THE AFTERMATH OF ACTEAL

In the days following the massacre, national and international outrage provided the pressure that people like Alonso needed to be able to return to their communities and rescue their families. Five days after the massacre, in the predawn hours of December 27, Alonso—accompanied by human rights organizations and protected by the Mexican Judicial Police—returned to Los Chorros, where his family was being held hostage by paramilitary members. As his wife and children began to leave, other families asked to be rescued. More than 300 people left Los Chorros that day.

Also because of national and international pressure, steps have been taken to bring some of the perpetrators of the crime to justice in this case. In 1999, 44 indigenous people, including the PRI party mayor of Chenalho', were sentenced to 35 years in prison for participating in the massacre. The Attorney General's office indicated that another 86 people could be prosecuted. In May 1999, a retired Army general and two senior security police were also sentenced to eight years in prison for failing to intervene to stop the attack.[24] In Decem-

---

[24]Reuters, July 8, 2000.

© Jess Hunter

ber 1999, two former state government officials were sentenced to six years in prison for having protected the paramilitary group who carried out the massacre. A former Public Ministry agent, Roberto Arcos Jiménez, was convicted of not having acted against the civilians who were arming themselves in the area, while former first officer of the Public Security Police, Absalon Gordillo Díaz, was convicted of carrying firearms restricted to the use of the Army.[25]

One interesting case that has not been brought to trial is that of Julio César Ruíz Ferro, who was the Governor of Chiapas at the time

---

[25]SIPAZ Report, March 2000.

of the massacre. Ruíz is accused of "homicide by omission" in the case of Acteal. The charges are: 1) that he knew of the existence of the paramilitary groups; 2) that he was informed of their being trained by government forces (and might have had something to do with actually providing the guns); 3) that he was informed of the threats of the massacre; 4) that he was called several times during the course of the seven hour massacre; and 5) that he did not respond in any way either by intervening or by ordering investigations into these types of denunciations. There is no case against Ruíz Ferro at this time, however. He is enjoying diplomatic immunity as the agricultural attaché at the Mexican Embassy in Washington, DC.[26]

Today, the primary intellectual authors of the Acteal massacre and their accomplices at the various levels of local, state and federal government are still free. Furthermore, while paramilitary violence continues, there is still no official recognition of the existence of paramilitary groups or of their connection to the government.

The aftermath of Acteal did not bring peace to Chenalho' or provide the displaced *Abejas* with a way to return home. Using the Acteal massacre as an excuse to militarize the region even further, the government sent 5,000 more soldiers to Chiapas. Of these, 2,000 were sent to reinforce the soldiers already stationed in Chenalho'. They were not sent to the communities where the aggressors live, but rather to the areas where the victims of the violence had sought refuge. As a result, there is about one soldier for every ten inhabitants in the municipality of Chenalho'.[27] The government claims they are there to protect the displaced people and to provide medical care and other social services. Thus, with the excuse of preventing another massacre, the government moved into new positions and went on the offensive to continue the low-intensity war.

---

[27]Estimates of CIEPAC, the Center for Research and Education for Peace in Chiapas. www.ciepac.org
[26]*La impunidad Reina: El ex-Gobernador de Chiapas, implicado en la masacre de Acteal, goza de la impunidad en Washington, D.C.*, Fray Bartolomé Human Rights Center.

The number of displaced people in Chenalho' today is calculated to be 10,000. This is a huge figure given that the total municipal population is only about 30,000. The displaced continue to live in conditions of extreme poverty and psychological anguish because of their separation from their land, their dependence on outside aid, and because of constant threats and harassment by the Army, the State Public Security Police and other security forces, as well as by members of paramilitary groups who continue to operate in the area.

In mid-2000, it was estimated that there were some 60,000 Mexican Army troops in Chiapas.[28]

---

[28]Ibid.

✳

# EPILOGUE

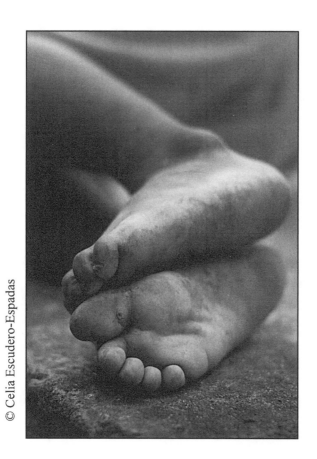

# CHIAPAS, MEXICO: 1997-2001

The situation in Chiapas deteriorated dramatically after the Acteal massacre and after I finished gathering testimonies for this book in December of 1997. Militarization increased, and security forces began to launch direct attacks on autonomous communities. In 1998, the Chiapas state government launched a military campaign against communities in the rainforest and *Las Cañadas*, dismantling autonomous governments in several municipalities such as Taniperlas and Amparo Aguatinta. The work of international observers also became more difficult in 1998 when Mexico's Department of Immigration began to deport more foreigners.[1] Due to the lack of good-faith participation on the part of the government, peace negotiations stagnated completely. Bishop Samuel Ruíz resigned as president of the National Intermediation Commission (CONAI), and CONAI disbanded.

In November 1999, Samuel Ruíz—then 75 years old—retired as Bishop of San Cristóbal de las Casas. Most Catholics in Chiapas expected his successor to be Raúl Vera, who had been Ruíz's ally and the Adjunct Bishop of San Cristóbal from 1995 to 1999. In a surprise move from the Vatican, however, Vera was removed from Chiapas and sent to Saltillo in northern Mexico. Instead, Felipe Arizmendi—previously the Bishop of Tapachula—became the new Bishop of San Cristóbal. Arizmendi is more theologically conservative than Ruíz or Vera, but so far he has taken social positions in favor of the indigenous and the poor, and he has not chosen to dismantle the pastoral work set in place by Bishop Ruíz.

Other important changes have also occurred recently, changes that may forever alter the balance of power in Chiapas. On July 2, 2000 a non-PRI candidate—Vicente Fox of the PAN party—won the national presidential elections, and on August 20, 2000 the governorship of Chiapas also went to an opposition coalition. Thus it seems

---

[1]Since 1995, some 400 foreigners have been expelled from Chiapas for allegedly violating their tourist visas by participating in "political activities." Michael Flynn, *The Bulletin of the Atomic Scientists,* September-October 2000, p. 47.

that the dominance of the PRI party may be ending at both federal and state levels. There is no doubt that this is the result of decades of struggle for democratic change—a struggle which includes union organizing, student movements, agrarian conflicts and the formation of new opposition parties. There has also been a change in the consciousness of a great majority of Mexican people who no longer believe in a one-party government. They understand their rights, feel more independent in their electoral choices and are willing to struggle to achieve democratic change.

These new changes are also, in part, the result of the struggle of the indigenous people of Chiapas.

One could say that the Zapatista insurrection of 1994 and the struggle of the indigenous people of Chiapas have been positive influences on the general population of Mexico. After all, if poor indigenous people in the poorest state of Mexico are willing to risk their lives and the little they have in a struggle for civil rights and democracy, why then, would urban middle class citizens not give up their own fear and indifference and go out to vote for the changes they feel Mexico needs?

The election of Vicente Fox as President of Mexico—the first non-PRI president in over 70 years—is the direct outcome of this new sense of empowerment. But, as many analysts have pointed out, Fox's election was less a function of the PAN's center-right platform and more the result of a general disenchantment with the PRI and a desire for change. The need to resolve the conflict in Chiapas also played an important role during the presidential campaign. Vicente Fox's promises to return the government to the negotiation table and to get the army out of the Chiapas were strong points in his favor. They may have helped offset his PRI-like positions of support for neoliberal economic policies and a general disinterest in the plight of the rural poor.

It is too soon to predict whether the war will end or whether poverty will be alleviated in Chiapas as a result of the new government. As this book goes to press, there are some positive changes occurring. When Fox took office on December 1, 2000, he immediately ordered the dismantling of 53 military checkpoints in Chiapas.

He also reiterated his pledge to send the San Andrés Accords to Congress to be signed. The EZLN responded the next day with an openness to renewed peace talks with the new government. Their preconditions to new talks include the release of Zapatista political prisoners and the closing of important military bases in Chiapas. Sub-commander Marcos also announced the EZLN's intention to send its military command to Mexico City in February or March to lobby Congress for the approval of the San Andrés Accords.

Given the obstacles, it is hard to know how optimistic to be about these changes. In most cases, the dismantling of checkpoints ordered by Fox meant that the soldiers simply retreated to their camps at the side of the road. However, even this minimal action did result in a significant change in the lives of many indigenous people who no longer had to face interrogation and harassment on a daily basis. In addition, President Fox has ordered the closure of four of the seven military bases identified by the EZLN and has released a few Zapatista prisoners. The approval of the San Andrés Accords in congress is uncertain, as the legislation is likely to face competing proposals in the new Congress. Anything other than the original legislative proposal is likely to be unacceptable to the EZLN.

The state government in Chiapas is also going through important changes. Pablo Salazar Mendiguchía, the opposition coalition candidate, is now the governor of Chiapas. Salazar is a former PRI senator and a founding member of the Commission of Concord and Pacification (COCOPA), the legislative body created to oversee the implementation of the peace accords. In 1997, he challenged the federal executive for its refusal to implement the San Andrés Accords and eventually resigned from the PRI over the matter. Salazar is a Presbyterian with close connections to both evangelical Protestants and the Catholic Diocese. He is respected by opposition sectors, has a reputation for honesty and integrity and has a solid base in Chiapas. The coalition that supported his candidacy is diverse, however, including the PAN, the leftist PRD and the Worker's Party (PT) who came together for the first time in history to defeat the PRI. The state legislature and judicial system is still dominated by the PRI.

The challenges for the new governor are many. There is still an environment of violence, and conflicts exist over religious, political and economic differences in and among communities. Paramilitary groups that have been armed and trained by groups related to the PRI party are still active. In addition, there is the powerful system of local PRI politicians and rural economic elites who want the state to be governed as their private plantation. But a waning of PRI party dominance on the national scene may help to undercut the power of these groups.

Pablo Salazar will have to govern with strength and determination in order to make the changes that are necessary to overhaul the failed political system and begin to resolve the state's economic and social problems. He will have to work together with the people of Chiapas to create an environment of nonviolence, tolerance, and respect in order to achieve the reconciliation, peace and justice needed for the development of the state.[2]

What then, will be the future for the autonomous communities in the rainforest, *Las Cañadas* and the highlands? What will happen to the internal refugees of northern Chiapas and Chenalho'? What will be the situation for the Mayan people in San Cristóbal de las Casas?

At the present time, there is still no real possibility that the displaced people living in the camps of Polho' and Xoyep (where the *Abejas* live) will return soon to their communities in Chenalho'. Several times the *Abejas* have thought about returning, and every time, they have decided to wait for better conditions. Alonso, for example, continues to live in San Cristóbal de las Casas with his family. He knows that his return to Los Chorros could mean his death. And yet, he is better off than the thousands of displaced who live in horrible conditions in Polho' and Xoyep.

There are great obstacles to the return of the displaced. One of them is that members of paramilitary groups are still living in their communities. The other is that the majority of displaced people have

---

[2]Information from ALIANZA 2000, #2, January 2000 and "Chiapas Elections," by Teresa Ortiz, June 2000 *Utopías.*

lost their homes. Only serious actions from both federal and state governments could create the necessary conditions in the communities for them to return. These actions would have to include disarming the paramilitary groups, bringing to trial all the material and intellectual authors of human rights violations including the Acteal massacre and other assassinations, getting the army away from the civilian communities and restoring an environment of peace. The victims of the war must have help to rebuild their homes and replace their belongings, and restitution must be paid to the families of those who have been assassinated. In addition, an environment of trust must be created to facilitate a return to the negotiation table.

Even if the government does take strong action and even if the EZLN and the government do return to the negotiation table, it will still be a long process to establish an environment of peace and reconciliation in the communities. A particularly difficult case is in the northern zone, which continues to be extremely tense and critical. And yet, despite all of this, a quiet hope is emerging in the communities of Chiapas, particularly in the autonomous regions. The Zapatista people and other independent indigenous groups continue to struggle at the local level to develop their communities, to grow in their movement of autonomy, and to achieve peace with justice, dignity and democracy.

The Mayan people's tradition of resistance and struggle under terrible conditions is an example for the people of Mexico and the world. This is a great moment for Chiapas and for Mexico, a pregnant time of hope and expectation as well as a very difficult time of struggle. In this context a great challenge faces the international solidarity movement as well. We need to support the people of Chiapas in their efforts to achieve their long awaited peace with justice, to reconstruct their lives and communities, and to continue in their struggle for democracy, civil rights and autonomy. There is so much for all of us to do. We have heard the stories of the people of Chiapas. We must not abandon them during these difficult times.

# APPENDICES

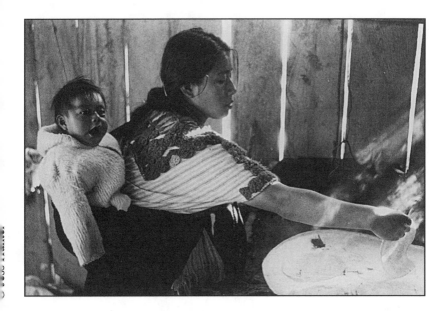

# A NEW CYCLE OF LIFE FOR THE MAYAN PEOPLE

## By Oscar Hernández[1]

In the first early hours of 1994, an indigenous army descended in mass from the mountains into the cities of Chiapas, Mexico and into world consciousness. In a document called the *Declaration of the Lacandona Jungle*, Subcomandante Marcos and a band of short, dark, "sickly" Indians armed with AK-47s, .22 caliber pigeon rifles and wooden sticks declared war on Mexico's "illegitimate government" and said, "Enough is Enough!" Their audacity seemed surreal. Yet, after ten days of bombardment by the Mexican Army, the rebels— members of the Zapatista Army of National Liberation (EZLN)— were able to achieve a cease-fire and begin negotiations with the government. National and international opinion had convinced the image-conscious, Mexican government and ruling Institutional Revolutionary Party (PRI) to come to the table. And the world had discovered Chiapas—*El Mundo Maya.*

The Mayans are a spiritual people. They and other Mesoamerican peoples believe that theirs is one of many universes that had existed before and that would eventually be destroyed, only to give rise to another universe and begin the cycle of creation and life once again. But just as the Mayan cycle repeats itself approximately every 5,200 years, modern Mexican history is also a cycle of life death and rebirth. The Zapatistas are part of this history.

For many people unfamiliar with Mexican history, Mexico is an exotic paradise. It is a peaceful third-world country that has been spared the political violence that swept most Latin American nations after World War II. Mexico is sunny beaches in Acapulco and Cancún,

---

[1]This article appears with the author's permission.

tequila, *mariachis*, the Mexican Hat dance and colorful customs and costumes. On January 1, 1994 the Zapatistas cracked this image.

Then, for many people unfamiliar with Mexico, the Zapatistas became the strange and wonderful guerrillas, the first post-Cuban rebellion in exotic Mexico, the pacifist, Mayan guerrillas. The Zapatistas' poetic entrance onto the world stage was the "noble savage's" mystical entrance into the new millennium—the coming of a new age.

Yet the Zapatista rebellion is even more remarkable than that. It is an integral part of the Mexicans' struggle for life in a system plagued with injustice. It is a rebirth of the popular movement destroyed in the 60s. It is 5200 Mayan years compressed into a quarter century.

Twenty-five years before the world discovered Marcos, a man named Lucio Cabañas led another movement in the mountains of the Sierra de Atoyac in the state of Guerrero. At that time, poor *campesino* and indigenous people were organizing peaceful marches and meetings to protest their living conditions. State security forces responded by opening fire on them. Seeing the toll of dead and injured, Lucio Cabañas—a rural schoolteacher of humble origins—came to the conclusion that only an armed rebellion would make their voices heard.

Lucio's group was never more than a ragtag army of a few hundred armed guerrillas, but it did have the support of many impoverished communities. It took the Mexican Army and its US-advised, Vietnam-inspired scorched-earth policy seven years to defeat them. And this was without the world's eyes, without human rights observers and with a much more cowardly press. In the end, however, the Guerrero rebellion was suppressed, and little was changed to resolve the underlying social problems.

Today, the Mexican government is seeking a military solution to its insurgency problem once again. The EZLN is poorly armed, yet thousands strong. According to US and Mexican government intelligence reports, there are about a dozen insurgent groups in Guerrero, Oaxaca, Chiapas and other states. How long will it take to suppress these new uprisings and achieve the solution sought by the Mexican government and its World Bank advisors? How many more cycles of destruction and rebirth must pass before the elite realize that as long as the social and economic conditions of Mexico do not change, these rebellions will not disappear?

*El que nada debe, nada teme*— "A person with a clean conscience has nothing to fear"—goes a popular Mexican saying. But now, three decades after Lucio's rebellion, Mexico is striving to present itself as a modern "first world" country, and it's feeling a bit uncomfortable. National and international human rights observers, United Nations Special Rapporteurs, solidarity groups and NGOs are all witnesses to how the Mexican government will choose to respond to social unrest within its borders. Even as "modern" Mexico incorporates itself into the New Financial World Order, these groups come and visit the other Mexico: the indigenous Mexico, the Mexico of the poor struggling for justice.

On February 9, 1995, the Zapatista command was waiting in the jungle town of Guadalupe Tepeyac for the government negotiating team to continue with the dialogue begun the previous year. They were met, however, by the arrival of tanks, soldiers, and police intent on their arrest. Marcos and his insurgent colleagues managed to escape as the army occupied the jungle towns, harassing and displacing thousands of civilian Zapatista sympathizers.

This military offensive failed to decapitate the Zapatista movement, but it allowed the Mexican Army to advance its positions. At the same time the army was establishing these new jungle positions, the nation's desire for a peaceful solution to the conflict was being written into legislation in the *Law for Dialogue, Reconciliation and a Dignified and Just Peace in Chiapas*. This established the legal basis for the dialogue between the federal government and the EZLN. From that moment on, in order to protect its image in the public eye, the government, army and police forces decided on a strategy that would make their role in counterinsurgency less visible. Putting to use training from the US Army School of the Americas, they organized paramilitary groups who would wage a war of attrition against the enemy.

Through this new strategy, the Mexican Army began a more discrete war that would permit the government to plausibly deny its complicity in human rights violations and atrocities. The *Manual of*

*Irregular War* by the Mexican National Defense Secretary mentions "operations to control the population" which include, among other measures, the "organization of control forces" and "the training of forces (civilian military and militarized)." Paramilitary groups were formed to diminish the organizational strength of the opposition through the intimidation and displacement of civilian populations. This strategy was applied first in the Ch'ol region bordering the State of Tabasco in northern Chiapas. This region has been plagued by paramilitary violence since early 1995, when the group cynically named Paz y Justicia (Peace and Justice) first appeared on the scene. Its objective was to destroy communities that opposed the government and to expel from pro-government communities those who did not share their ideas. Within the complex picture of the region, one thing that is obvious is the illicit complicity between *Paz y Justicia* and the Chiapan police forces.

In March of 1995, one month after the government's offensive, the first reports of paramilitary violence in the Ch'ol region of Tumbalá reached the San Cristóbal office of the Fray Bartolomé de Las Casas Human Rights Center. By June and July, *Paz y Justicia* had attacked the lowlands of Tila, and by August the violence had spread to the municipality of Sabanilla.

In September, Paz y Justicia reinitiated attacks in the municipalities of Tila, Tumbalá and Salto de Agua in order to paralyze the opposition—Party of the Democratic Revolution (PRD)—in the local election October 15. The attacks caused the massive displacement of PRD sympathizers, and Paz y Justicia members running on the PRI ticket won the elections, which were marked by high absenteeism.

The second peak of violence in the Cho'l region occurred between June and September of 1996. During this time, in July, the Fray Bartolomé de Las Casas Human Rights Center sent a brigade of 13 national and international observers to the northern zone to document the situation in the various communities with displaced people. On July 17, 1996, 17-year-old Mateo Vázquez Sánchez was ambushed and killed shortly after having given his testimony to the brigade.

A similar situation occurred again a year and a half later. On

February 21, 1998, José Tila López García was ambushed and killed almost immediately after having talked about paramilitary violence to international human rights observers. In both cases eyewitnesses named members of the paramilitary group *Paz y Justicia* as the perpetrators. To this day there have been hundreds of deaths from the violence that erupted in 1995 as part of the new government strategy. The region has more than 1,500 displaced people, and a paramilitary group physically dominates the roads of Tila and Sabanilla. The police forces, the Mexican military and the national government are allowing paramilitary groups to de facto govern four municipalities in northern Chiapas, and the fact that they commit abuses on a daily level has not been enough for any action to be taken against them.

Once northern Chiapas was under control, paramilitary violence—designed to geographically divide the area of Zapatista influence—descended 50 kilometers south to the municipality of Chenalho', the heart of the central Chiapas highlands.

In the wake of the ensuing violence, including the brutal massacre in Acteal, Mexican government authorities have insisted that the Zapatistas are to blame because they founded autonomous municipalities in the area. They claim that this inevitably led to conflicts between the PRI-led municipality in Chenalhó and the autonomous municipality of Polhó. What they do not mention is the fact that this conflict should have been dealt with politically through dialogue as specified in the *Law for Dialogue, Reconciliation and a Dignified Peace in Chiapas*—a law to which President Zedillo claimed to be personally committed. They also do not mention that they themselves sabotaged the attempts at dialogue.

In August 1996, a group of PRI-members threw six young men, sons of Zapatista sympathizers into a 100-meter-deep pit, yelling, "They're Zapatistas! They're Zapatistas!" This crime, like so many others in Chenalhó and in the rest of Chiapas, remains unpunished. Instead, it was used as a pretext to substitute the then municipal president with Jacinto Arias Cruz, a PRI hard-liner, who at all times has opted to resolve conflict with force and violence.

Jacinto Arias Cruz is currently in prison for his participation in the Acteal massacre. Unfortunately, he was one of the scapegoats used to try to distract the public from the complicity of higher level authorities. After the massacre, the authorities recognized the participation of Arias Cruz in the trafficking and the distribution of high-power weapons to PRI-affiliated paramilitary groups in the municipality. These facts were denounced for many months before the massacre, but were conveniently ignored by government officials.

With the support of Jacinto Arias Cruz, paramilitary members began to threaten anyone who did not want to collaborate with them. This included not only Zapatistas, and *Abejas*, but also other PRI members who opposed the paramilitary violence. The paramilitary threats and attacks provoked what is now one of the major human and political problems in the municipality of Chenalhó: the displacement of one-third of the population of the municipality out of fear for their lives.

The number of displaced people today is calculated to be 10,000 in a municipality that has a population of 30,000. The displaced live in conditions of extreme poverty and psychological anguish because of constant threats and harassment by the Army, the State Public Security Police (PSP) and the paramilitary members who remain free and unpunished.

On December 22, 1997, a group of displaced people were attacked in Acteal, a place they had gone to for refuge. There, at 10:30 AM, a heavily armed group of men affiliated with the PRI party attacked 300 unarmed people who belonged to a pacifist group called *Las Abejas.* One hour after the shooting began, the Diocese received a call from the public phone in Acteal reporting the shooting which could still be heard in the background. (The phone was about 100 meters from where the massacre was taking place.) One of Bishop Ruíz's vicars then called the Secretary of the State Government to inform him about what was happening in Acteal and to ask for his urgent intervention.

According to the Assistant Secretary Uriel Jarquín: "At 11:30 a.m. I received a call… I took note and informed him that we had no report at this moment. We immediately notified the Public Security Police stationed in the vicinity to verify. They found no evidence of a confrontation, no houses burnt down, no problem in the region which they reported to us. We reinforced the patrols and remained attentive." At that very moment paramilitary members were attacking unarmed people. The PSP was about 100 meters away from where the massacre took place. Acteal neighbors alerted the PSP of the shooting, but the PSP did not enter the community until after 5:00 p.m., more than six hours after the attack began and five hours after the vicar's call.

To add to the outrage, the government's National Human Right's Commission later reported that the intelligence service of the Ministry of the Interior had already informed the Secretary of the State Government that the killing was taking place in Acteal, even before the vicars' phone call.

Although *Las Abejas* did not put up armed resistance, the shooting lasted until 6:00 that evening. Forty-five people were killed, and 26 more were injured. Most of the victims were children. A few weeks after the massacre, when the majority of the perpetrators were still free, they even took the liberty of plundering the houses of those who fled Acteal. Two years after the massacre, the survivors of the attack and other displaced people continue to receive threats from paramilitary members, as the displacement of eleven families on November 1999 illustrates. None of the intellectual authors of the massacre have been arrested and some of the material perpetrators remain free as well.

Did the Mexican government's behavior show its complicity or its incompetence? The day after the massacre, the media questioned then Secretary of State, Emilio Chuayffet. Why had the government not done anything to prevent the massacre, given that the military, the police and the National Intelligence Service were present before and during the massacre? The public official responded that "events like the one on December 22 can escape any information system." Yet in the weeks preceding the massacre, a Mexican national television program denounced the violence in the municipality and demanded an urgent solution to avoid a tragedy. The program was watched by millions of spectators all over the country. One sector of the media repeated the denunciations almost daily. Members of CONAI (the mediating group in the stalled Zapatista-Government dialogue) insisted that a bloodbath could be foreseen. Also telling is the fact that at the time of the massacre, the PSP were stationed on the road that would have been the only escape for the victims. The aforementioned *Manual of Irregular War* clearly describes a "Hammer and Anvil Encirclement" annihilation operation. This maneuver corresponds to the tactic used in Acteal where the paramilitary members played the role of the hammer and the police were the block force that played the role of the anvil. The first action taken by the Government after the massacre was to send 5,000 more soldiers to Chiapas. Two thousand of these 5,000 were sent to reinforce the soldiers already stationed in Chenalhó. They were not sent to the communities where the aggressors live, but rather to the areas near where the victims of the violence had sought refuge, in an encircling operation also described in *Manual of Irregular War.* As a result, there is about one soldier for every ten inhabitants in the municipality of Chenalhó. The government claims they are there to protect the displaced people and to provide medical care and other social services. Thus, with the excuse of preventing another massacre, the government moved into new positions, mounted a low-intensity war, and went on the offensive.

The offensive continued throughout the first half of the following year, but in 1998, paramilitary groups took a back seat to the Bases of Mixed Operation (BOM). The BOM were composed of members of the Mexican Armed Forces together with state and federal police, and often, immigration officials.

The paramilitary groups did not disappear, however. Rather, they collaborated with the BOM forces in their attacks against autonomous Zapatista municipalities. To prepare for these attacks, an anti-foreigner campaign was begun to justify the illegal expulsion of human rights observers. This was accompanied by a defamation campaign against the Diocese of San Cristóbal de Las Casas, Bishop Samuel Ruíz and CONAI, of which Samuel Ruíz was the president.

On April 8, 1998, a predawn BOM operation took place in the San Cristóbal de Las Casas indigenous neighborhood of La Hormiga. In an overwhelming use of force, thousands of armed personnel were used to arrest several sleepy "criminals." With this success, the BOM were ready to attack Zapatista communities. At dawn on April 11, 1998, thousands of army troops, police officers and masked paramilitary members attacked the community of Taniperla, arrested a dozen community members and several Mexican human rights observers, and deported another dozen foreign human rights observers. The attacks continued in May with similar operations in Amparo, Agua Tinta, Navil and Nicolás Ruíz. At the same time, the government's defamation of Samuel Ruíz and the CONAI was such that on June 7, Bishop Ruíz resigned, and the next day the CONAI disbanded. The governor of Chiapas could not contain his glee as he publicly stated that "with the dissolution of the CONAI we are closer to peace." The governor's notion of peace was made clear just a few days later. On June 10, 1998, in the most bloody of all the operations against the autonomous communities, at least eight *campesinos* and two police officers lost their lives in the BOM attack of El Bosque.

But the national and international attention caused by the killings in El Bosque forced the government to change the emphasis of its low-intensity war once again. With visits from the Pope, the United Nation's Special Rapporteur on Summary Executions and finally the United Nation's High Commissioner on Human Rights, the government turned to publicity campaigns and the use of economic resources for counterinsurgency purposes. Under this new plan, the government stepped up its spending on military infrastructure such as roads, calling it economic development for the indigenous communities.

It is exactly this sort of road that is currently being unanimously opposed by a community called Amador Hernández at the edge of the Montes Azules Biosphere in the Lacandón jungle. This road would originate in the largest military encampment of the jungle, San Quintín. The San Quintín military camp, a permanent concrete construction with an asphalt airstrip, contrasts dramatically with the thatch-roofed wooden homes of Ejido Emiliano Zapata only a few meters away.

The government bragged that they were closer to peace. But the closer we get to the government's peace, the farther we stray from the peace sought by the indigenous communities of Chiapas. Their peace means living with respect and without fear. It means being able to be part of the decisions that affect their lives and their community's development. The government's peace, on the other hand, is one of absolute political and economic control. It may be a peace without bullets, but it is replete with social, economic and political violence.

The current struggle of Chiapas' marginalized communities are the hope of an ageless people in their continuing struggle for dignity—a struggle which will doubtless involve more cycles of destruction and rebirth for as many times as is necessary for a life with dignity to be accompanied by justice.

San Cristóbal de las Casas
Chiapas, Mexico, June 2000

# WOMEN AND LOW-INTENSITY WARFARE[2]

Media reports on Chiapas often neglect the fact that behind the certainly alarming statistics (the result of the violence and the ever more worrisome dimensions of poverty, malnutrition, illiteracy, etc.), there are beings of flesh and blood, families and communities that are struggling to survive.

The cease-fire of January 1994 has not meant an end to the violence. The conflict between the government and the EZLN has continued and been extended in the form of an increasingly complex low intensity war: militarization and paramilitary groups, divisions in organizations and communities, an information war (via everything from rumors to the mass media), etc. This counter-insurgency strategy seeks to "take away the water from the fish," the EZLN being the fish and civil society, as a source of material and intellectual support, whether actual or potential, being the water.

In this context, the already critical situation of Indian women in Chiapas has deteriorated. But the reality of their daily lives is little known. Here we offer a space for the heart of these women to speak and to hear their voice, as victims of low intensity warfare and as protagonists who seek to control their own lives and to contribute to the peace process.

## How Low-Intensity Warfare Affects Women

### As Human Beings

The biggest impact on the life of the women is the fact that, because of the presence of the Mexican army in their communities, their activities are restricted. They are afraid to go to the corn fields,

---

[2]From *SIPAZ Bulletin*, January 1998. Reprinted with permission from International Service for Peace (SIPAZ).

to the river to bathe or wash clothes, to gather firewood or to sell their handicrafts.

Women from Comitán and Las Margaritas complain of the military checkpoints: "They stop us, they ask for our identification and for information about the Zapatistas, about the catechists in our communities, etc." In fact, checkpoints and patrols, both military and paramilitary, are part of daily life in many parts of Chiapas. A woman from Tila tells us her story: "We are hungry because we can't work. We can't go out to buy what we need. They [the paramilitary group called 'Peace and Justice'] are armed, so we cannot defend ourselves. They won't allow us to leave. They are there, watching the road, in a truck with their guns. And they continue arming and arming the people."

Another point to consider is that frequently, the women are the most exposed because they are the ones who stay in the communities with the children and the elderly when the men flee to the mountains. They are the ones who show their face. Among the murdered in the December 22 massacre in Acteal in the municipality of Chenalho' were 21 women—four of them pregnant.

### As Women

The conflict impacts women in a distinct manner. As Marta Figueroa of the Women's Group of San Cristóbal underscores, "The question of gender is almost invisible. It isn't even thought about, but it has always been like that in war. Women are a privileged channel for the reproduction of fear." Mercedes Olivera of CIAM (Center for Investigation and Support for Women) adds that women are seen as "objects and as military objectives" in the sense that they are the ones "who give life to the next generation of guerrillas" and in some sense represent "the means to defeat the populace." In fact, actions against women are aimed at frightening and dispiriting not only them, but also the whole community.

### Harassment and Rape

Threats of a sexual nature are quite common. According to women's groups in San Cristóbal, there are many cases of harassment and rape, but for the most part they are not reported. Rosalinda (in a workshop of indigenous women) explained to us one of the reasons for this silence: "The violence is lived in silence, and it echoes in our physical health. We also redirect it against ourselves, since we feel guilty. Violence and submission are learned."

## Terror and Rumors

In one of their meetings, the women of CODIMUJ (Diocesan Coordinating Committee for Women) realized that the thing that most divides the communities is rumors. Tere gives us an example of how rumors generate confusion and finally disinformation: "Another thing is the rumors that go around. It is the means of information for the people. For example, my mother asked me yesterday if it is true that they pay people to be in the 'Peace Belts' [protection offered by civil society during the talks between the EZLN and the Mexican government.]"

These rumors feed a climate of tension that sometimes borders on paranoia. In many communities, troop movements heighten these anxieties. (Might that be one of their functions?) Juana from Amatenango del Valle expresses her fears: "The government really doesn't want dialogue. The PRI supporters say that there is going to be war. So I believe that there is going to be war."

## Prostitution

Another form of violence against women is the growth of prostitution. Many 16 or 17-year-old prostitutes are Central Americans who entered the country illegally without immigration officials seeming to mind. However, there are also growing numbers of cases of indigenous women who "go with the soldiers." They pay 100 *pesos* for virgins, 50 *pesos* for the others. The prettiest are "reserved" for high-ranking officers. It seems that the soldiers deceive them with promises or that they are convinced by the misery of the situation in which they and their families live. There are also some cases of child prostitution, of 11- to 13-year-old girls sold or "loaned" by their fathers in order to alleviate situations of hunger. This causes great dishonor in the communities (unfortunately, for the girl, not for the father).

## Health

Parallel to the prostitution, there has been a growth in sexually transmitted diseases, and some cases of AIDS have been identified. Marta Figueroa of the Women's Group of San Cristóbal commented, "For the most part, the soldiers reject the use of condoms. On some occasions, in workshops to promote awareness, they threw them on the ground in a flaunting manner." According to the testimony of women's organizations from San Cristóbal, the tension generated by the conflict is even reflected in the kinds of sicknesses that the indigenous people display, illnesses that at times are of a psychosomatic character, such as gastritis, headaches, etc. Another related theme is the control that can be exercised through the provision of health services. "We have seen the pressure on many indigenous women who have come seeking medical services. There is always a big interrogation about whether they are Zapatistas or not, where they are from, etc." (Yolanda, K'nal Antsetik, an organization that works with women's cooperatives in the Chiapas highlands).

### As Spouses and Mothers

The situation of constant conflict and economic crisis generates permanent anxiety among the populace. Among other manifestations, this is evidenced by an increase in domestic violence. "The violence affects all the families: some are the victims of it; others learn it and reproduce it." (Francisca, in a workshop of indigenous women.) In addition, the military presence brings with it a "barracks culture" that impacts negatively on the daily life of the communities and the families—alcoholism, drug addiction, or as we have seen, prostitution and its corollary, sexually transmitted diseases.

In difficult times, with an extraordinary degree of self-denial, the women express that "their mother's heart" is what tells them what to do when they see their children frightened, hungry, or sick. Naturally, one of their main concerns is the children's health. There are many children's diseases that, according to them, "nothing can be done about." However in reality, many of them are treatable. In 1994, Chiapas had the highest level of infant mortality in Mexico, with the principle cause of death being diarrhea. The women are also concerned with education: the lack of teachers, schools closed because of the conflict, or—in divided communities—schools where the Zapatista children can't go. Also, there is a growing number of children of soldiers. The mothers carry on under the most difficult emotional conditions because they are branded by the community. These situations evoke in these women either self-hatred or hatred against the community. Many turn to abortion as a form of self-punishment. According to Consuelo Lievano, the founder of Community Home "Yach'il Antzetik" (for pregnant women in difficult circumstances), the women will make comments like "now I must pay because I got involved [in prostitution]." She also emphasizes that since 1994, the number of abandoned children has risen.

Other mothers, members of CODIMUJ, expressed their concern for the sons who go to the prostitutes and then encourage their spouses and sisters to prostitute themselves. For others, the presence of a new source of employment that offers training and a guaranteed paycheck leads them to enlist in the army.

Divisions and conflicts in the home are another issues that "affect the heart." "There are a number of cases of women who accused their husbands—who are now in prison—with made up charges in order to protect their sons," says Mercedes Olivera of CIAM. Tere of Civic Alliance comments, "I have companions that had conflicts with their spouses or with their sons because the men wanted to carry on as before, that is, that the women would stay at home serving them. They didn't want to let them participate in something more open." Hilaria from Oxchuc, who had to flee her community because of political differences, told us about her case: "Before there were people from my family who did not speak to me; that is why I left. Now they don't hate me, and I go to visit them. There have been many quarrels in the families."

### As Housewives and/or Workers

As housewives, the women are responsible for the well-being—in this case more like the survival—of the family. It is ever more difficult to provide the minimum necessary, given the conjunction of two factors: the scarcity of production—agricultural production cycles disrupted in several areas and in many cases poor or inadequate land—and inflation of prices. In effect, with the presence of the soldiers alongside the communities, a "fictitious" economy has evolved. The women wash the soldiers' clothes and prepare tortillas and food for them. Sometimes they even open a little store with basic items. While in the short term they may benefit from this new source of investment, in the end it does not resolve the deeper problems, and it results in a rise in prices.

As the women of CODIMUJ express it: "Each day the peasant is poorer. He works a lot and his products never fetch a good price. They are almost given away. Our income buys less and less because of the rise in prices of gasoline, rice, sugar... everything." This is much more worrisome if we keep in mind that, according to the latest census, in Chiapas only 36.9% of the working population receives a minimum salary or more. The national average is 69.2%.

The situation is even more difficult for the thousands of displaced. In the northern region, for example, it is estimated that there are 4,100 displaced persons who are Zapatista sympathizers. In Chenalho' there are 5,000.[3] This consequence of violence in the communities particularly affects the women: "Being displaced takes away part of their identity, because the house is their life, where they express themselves as women. To destroy the pots and the clothes is also to destroy their personal environment."[4]

Finally, low intensity warfare affects the women as workers. There have been cases in which the army has set up camp right in their areas of production, for example, where they are growing vegetables. They lose their crops and all the time they invested. Other times, the few cattle that they have are stolen.

Yolanda, from K'nal Antsetik, tells us of the case of women shepherds in the highlands. "Because they were afraid to go out, little by little the women became detached from their sheep. Maybe it seems like something insignificant, but for them sheep are sacred animals,

---

[3] In the year 2000, the number of displaced in Chenalho' rose to 10,000.
[4] Mercedes Olivera, CIAM

almost like their children. It is connected to their weaving work. This took both an economic and an emotional toll... I could see their worries reflected in the quality of their weavings. After February 1995, the quality went down, and ever since it has been difficult to regain it."

Since that time, with the entrance of the army into the communities and the polarization that this caused, the divisions also began to get worse in the women's groups. Whether or not to accept aid from the government—even if it is minimal—has been and continues to be another source of polarization.

## Women Who Take Their Destiny Into Their Own Hands

In this context of low intensity warfare, we should recognize the bravery of many indigenous women. They are small and short, bent over with a big load of firewood, or with their youngest child on their back, but what strength is evident in their eyes! Alma, advisor in CODIMUJ, comments, "In spite of the situation that is very conflictive in several areas, the women continue to meet, although never in large groups. Such security measures are necessary in particular in the northern region. Paradoxically, participation has even grown since 1994."

At the beginning, it seems that the Zapatista rebellion was "like a spark, a wake-up call, an effervescence where more organized women's groups were born," according to Yolanda, K'nal Antsetik. They began to participate more openly in marches, in road blockades, in the autonomous municipalities, Amatenango del Valle, for example.

In the peace process, during the dialogues, the women were present, not only in the Peace Belts but also in the community level discussions of the issues and even at the peace table.

Regarding the Peace Belts, Tere recalls, "The men take on the question of force, but in the support of the movement, the majority are women. I feel it is because it is how we are. We are more disciplined, and we really take hold of our tasks. We take charge of the essential. This represents a lot of work, but it has a great deal of human value. The people remember you as 'mother and benefactor.'"

Recently, women have again demonstrated their courage by participating in several demonstrations. At the end of August in San Cayetano, when the military camp was reinstalled, women were at the head of the protests. In Chenalho' at the end of November, several women were attacked when they formed a barrier to impede the access of the military. In that same municipality, a group was formed called the "Organization for the Rights of Women of San Pedro Chenalho'." It has been very active in denouncing the violence that they have suffered.

The women also try to create their own spaces through state-level gatherings called "Walking together toward peace." Other efforts to bring women together are undertaken in RECEPAC, a coordinating committee for handicrafts cooperatives with divergent political persuasions, or CODIMUJ. In a CODIMUJ meeting, one of the conclusions was that they should "Work for unity. This does not mean that we all belong to one single organization, but that we learn to work together."

In spite of the low intensity warfare and of its painful effects on the women, in Chiapas there has been an encouraging process of consciousness raising and hope. In the words of a 60-year-old woman who participated in the Peace Belts, " Since my eyes could see this hope for change, even if I die, I will die peacefully. Because for the first time I am seeing that this possibility exists, that things are moving."

SIPAZ Bulletin, January 1998

## ZAPATISTA REVOLUTIONARY WOMEN'S LAWS

In the just revolutionary struggle for the liberation of our people, the EZLN incorporates women, regardless of their race, creed, color or political affiliation, requiring only that they share the demands of the exploited people and that they commit to the laws and regulations of the revolution. In addition, because of the particular difficulties that women workers face in Mexico, the revolution supports their just demands for equality in the following Laws of Women.

*First:*

Women, regardless of their race, creed, color or political affiliation, have the right to participate in the revolutionary struggle in a way determined by their desire and capacity.

*Second:*

Women have the right to work and receive a just salary.

*Third:*

Women have the right to decide the number of children they will have and care for.

*Fourth:*

Women have the right to participate in the affairs of the community and to hold positions of authority if they are freely and democratically elected.

*Fifth:*

Women and their children have the right to primary attention in matters of health and nutrition.

*Sixth:*

Women have the right to education.

*Seventh:*

Women have the right to freely choose their partner, and should not be forced into marriage.

*Eighth:*

Women shall not be beaten or physically mistreated either by relatives or by strangers. Rape and attempted rape shall be severely punished.

*Ninth:*

Women will be able to occupy positions of leadership in the organizations and hold military ranks in the revolutionary armed forces.

*Tenth:*

Women will have the rights and obligations elaborated in the Revolutionary Laws and Regulations.

# WHOSE SIDE ARE WE ON?

## A Look at the US Role in Chiapas

### by Mara Kaufman

*We didn't see the Public Security checkpoint on the side of the road until we were almost upon it. Marisol braked quickly but their headlights captured us. I ducked down in the back of our old pickup and the 11 indigenous farmers—*campesinos*—in the back with me quickly shed their wool ponchos and threw them over me. I shrank lower under the heavy cloth and put my mouth down by the crack between the wood boards of the truck's floor to breathe.*

*"Buenas noches," one of the public security officers called out as we slowed to a stop. Five more officers emerged from the darkness and surrounded the pickup. "A dónde van?" Where are you going? We travel at night precisely to avoid the military, immigration and public security checkpoints that surround the indigenous communities. This one took us by surprise.*

*"Paseando," Marisol[4] says. Going for a drive? At midnight in the conflict zone? Their flashlights beam over the back of the truck, and even through the thick wool I see the light scan the campesino faces and pause on the lump that is me. "Todos mexicanos?" Everyone is Mexican? they ask. Here is the real reason we are stopped— are there foreigners in there, talking to the indigenous people, supporting their struggle, taking their story out of the jungle and down from mountains and out to the world? "Si, todos mexicanos," Marisol says. I hold my breath as the flashlight beams make another scan of the faces in the back of the truck. "Bueno, pase. Que les vaya bien," they say finally. Fine, go on, and go well.*

---

[4]Persons quoted here are not identified by name for their own safety.

I came to Chiapas in August of 1999, following the thousands of international volunteers before me that have come to this conflict zone since the Zapatista uprising. While the Zapatistas made their first public appearance via a small rebel army, their mass—and strength—is in the thousands of unarmed indigenous farmers in the Mexican countryside that make their demands for justice through word, work and peaceful resistance. It is these communities we come to support.

The call for international presence in Chiapas rang out over the world in 1995. The cease-fire between the EZLN and the Mexican army existing since January 12, 1994, was unilaterally broken by the Mexican government in a full military offensive against the indigenous communities. Soldiers invaded the villages, destroying houses and crops, beating, kidnapping, in some cases killing community leaders and displacing thousands of people. Churches, non-governmental organizations and Mexican civil society called for the eyes and ears of the world to come be witness to the atrocities that had been committed against not an army, but a civilian population.

*Why does a small rebel army, poorly armed, and a rural indigenous population, poorly fed, present such a threat to the Mexican government? It is not the armed guerilla in the mountains that those in power consider so dangerous; it is the power of a popular civilian movement. Their demands? Food, land, shelter. The most basic of human dignity. To be able to grow their corn and feed their children. They are those that have refused to be run over by a narrow definition of progress or to be rolled up neatly into the anonymous masses—those who have declared themselves in resistance.*

### Resistance

In 1993, in preparation for the passage of the North American Free Trade Agreement (NAFTA) and the subsequent demands of its neighbors to the north, Mexico changed Article 27 of its constitution, eliminating the land reform laws which had protected communally held indigenous lands, called *ejidos*, from being privatized or bought up by foreign investment or industry. The constitutional changes and new NAFTA regulations removed tariffs and subsidies protecting small farmers, promoting corporate interests and foreign investment and, in effect, impoverishing masses of rural Mexicans. January 1, 1994, NAFTA went into effect, as did the revolution. The Zapatista uprising stormed the Mexican southeast and the world's conscience with the words:

*Today we say enough! We are a product of 500 years of struggle... [W]e have been denied the most elemental education so that others can... pillage the wealth of our country... [W]e have nothing, absolutely nothing, not even a roof over our heads, no land, no work, no health care, no food, and no education... Nor is there peace and justice for us or our children.*

For the indigenous people in Chiapas, the struggle is about the creation of a just society. On a local level, that means taking control of their lives by designing their own sustainable economic development while maintaining traditional social and political customs. But they also work to build a civilian base—one that reaches far beyond Chiapas—that is conscious of economic and cultural oppression, that moves toward the construction of a society that is inclusive, just and democratic.

The communities in resistance refuse government aid so that they can't be pulled by the strings attached—the buying of votes, the dividing of communities through social services conditioned by party support, the meager handouts that keep people dependent yet underserved. One woman in the struggle explains, "A year ago, the government offered [us] ten dental clinics, but we said, 'Look, we didn't rebel to get ten dental clinics. We want dental care for the entire nation. We want education for all of Mexico. We don't want these services just for the indigenous people in Chiapas, we want them for everyone.'" In response to the lack of respect, recognition and rights denied them by their government, these communities have developed their own governing councils, education systems using their own languages, alternative health care and cultural centers. They have called on the international community not only to come and support them in the movement, but to take the struggle home, to wage battle for democracy in their own countries, states and communities. They do not fight to take power, but to empower.

### Low-Intensity War

After the 1995 military offensive, and with a few exceptions, the federal government changed its strategy. The investment interests and supposed human rights standards of Mexico's new northern partners in the free trade treaty made recognition of the popular momentum of the Zapatista movement politically dangerous and an open military attack on the indigenous communities impossible. For the past five years, the Mexican government—using the army, police and public security forces as tools—has engaged in a steady counterinsurgency war on the communities, funneling some 70,000 soldiers, 681 military camps and billions of dollars in tanks, helicopters and high caliber weapons into the state of Chiapas to repress the movement and "maintain order."

"Maintaining order" in this case means heavy militarization of areas of the state that are largely indigenous, mostly rural, and very, very poor. *La Jornada*, a national Mexican newspaper, printed in June of 1998:

*One of the strategies to wear these people down is to generate fear, to make those men and women who are conscious of their dignity, and who want to transform the injustice and the exclusion which they suffer, feel the weight of the power which confronts them and understand that the price for challenging this domination is death. The one who creates this psychological effect is, naturally, the Army.*[2]

Low-intensity war, or counterinsurgency, requires few bullets. It has no front lines nor trenches, because society is its battlefield. It makes violent attacks on social, political, economic, psychological and cultural levels. Intense militarization and paramiltarization (the training and arming of civilian groups by the military) create a psy-

---

[2]M. Concha. June 29, 1998

chological terror that make women too fearful too gather firewood and men too fearful to go to the fields. Media-controlled misinformation campaigns paralyze community organization through confusion, rumors and propaganda. The subsequent loss of productivity in addition to economic policies that undermine local production create a physical hunger and deepening poverty that leave people desperate enough to eat from the hand that holds them down or steal from their neighbor. Low-intensity war invades the political sector with fraud, impunity, manipulation and division. It invades culture through the destabilization of social structures and community relations, making a productive daily life difficult and peace of mind impossible.

Chiapas currently hosts one soldier for every 9 to 14 inhabitants in the conflict zone. This military presence has turned elementary schools into army barracks, young women into prostitutes and young men into paramilitary recruits. They have deforested the land, polluted the rivers and—through illegal evictions and terror tactics—displaced entire villages. There are presently 21,000 internal refugees in Chiapas.

The words of the community members reflect these conditions:

*We are sick with fright. Sometimes the soldiers come during the night and fire their guns in the road. Sometimes they come during the day when the men are away in the fields. They interrogate the women, demanding to know who the community leaders are, where they live, who their families are...*

*We can no longer drink from the river because the soldiers [defecate] in it... there is no wood for cooking because the trees have been cut down to build the army camps.*

*The government says there is no war. But we live as refugees... The aid they promise? It doesn't arrive. Sometimes the campaign cars come—those who vote for Labastida (the government party presidential candidate) get 500 pesos... The government says there aren't problems here, that we are fine. But they are telling public lies.*

The "party line," or official discourse, has been consistent: there is no war in Chiapas. "The only war in Chiapas is the government's war on poverty," states Emilio Rabasa Gamboa, Commissioner for the Dialogue for Peace in Chiapas. His statement, made in early June of 2000, nearly coincided with denunciations from Zapatista communities communicating their fear of imminent attack due to extremely tense conditions and increased military activity around their villages. Shortly before, and in the context of several recent ambushes in which 10 people were gunned down, Mexican President Ernesto Zedillo stated in a visit to Chiapas, "Social peace exists in this state. Recent violent acts have been an exception."

United States representatives have also claimed all is well in the state. Scarcely a year after the Acteal massacre in which 45 indigenous, mostly women and children, were shot down during a prayer service, and just six months after the massacre in El Bosque in which nine indigenous were grotesquely tortured and killed by police forces, US ambassador to Mexico Jeffrey Davidow stated, "I do not note signs of tension nor conflict. Everything seems very peaceful here."

### Whose Side Are We On?

Between 1997 and 1999 the US government provided over $112 million in military aid to Mexico to pay for arms, equipment and training. In addition to this aid, between 1996 and 1998 the State Department approved over $360 million in licenses for Direct Commercial Sales (DCS) of defense equipment to Mexico. More Mexican military personnel were trained in the United States in 1997 and 1998 than from any Latin American country—over 1,000 a year. The infamous School of the Americas trained almost as many Mexican officers in the first two years after the Zapatista uprising as it had in the previous 48 years.[3]

The majority of US money, weapons and training to Mexico comes earmarked for counter-narcotics purposes. But there are many doubts about their destiny. A United States Department of Defense

---

[3]S. Brian Wilson. www.globalexchange.org/campaigns/mexico/slope.

Inspector General's report revealed that the US military has spent millions of dollars over the past few years in increased surveillance and interdiction efforts in Mexico without any reduction in the flow of drugs from that country into the United States. In fact, the US State Department in 1996 assured the Zedillo administration that arms shipments did not have to be used exclusively for antidrug operations.[4] Between 1996 and 1997, while there were indeed Mexican military personnel taking antidrug courses at the School of Americas, three times as many were taking courses in counterinsurgency. And repeatedly, disclosed Pentagon documents point to the presence of US advisors and intelligence in Chiapas.[5] A January 14, 2000 letter to US Secretary of State, Madeleine Albright, signed by 15 members of the United States congress, states:

*We are concerned that US assistance intended for counter-narcotics programs is reportedly being used for other purposes, particularly counter-insurgency training for security forces and non-State, armed groups.*

So whose side are we on? United States investment funds, the import of US products and services by Mexico and the sale of energy sources—primarily oil—all make Mexico an issue of national security for the US government. According to the Mexican non-governmental organization, CIEPAC (Center for Economic and Political Research for Community Action), the Chiapas economy, along with that of Mexico in general, is oriented to foreign demand through two key arenas: an economic strategy geared toward direct foreign investment; and a plan for "combating poverty" using policies from the World Bank (and other multilateral organizations highly influenced by the US) to define Mexico's social spending policy.[6] Both of these policies have serious negative effects on Mexican rural areas and small farmers but are highly beneficial to US corporations and

---

[4]*La Jornada* May 17, 1996.
[5]S. Brian Wilson. www.globalexchange.org/campaigns/mexico/slope.
[6]See www.ciepac.org. Chiapas al Día. n.131.

big investors. Thus, according to the latter, any country—or citizens' movement—that resists the current free market policies, promotes alternative methods of development or reveals public unrest due to neoliberal policies, is a threat.

## Full Circle

In ironic contradiction to US military support of the Mexican military in Chiapas, United States citizens have responded in great numbers to the call by Mexican civil society for international presence and to the invitation by indigenous communities to accompany them in their struggle. In the words of one US observer:

*It is a responsibility I feel I have to recognize my government's role in oppression and to support a people who have the courage to confront their oppressors. This [the Zapatista movement] isn't a local issue. What they want—what they are fighting for—it is not just for them. It is for everyone.*

While heartily embraced in the indigenous communities, international observers are harshly treated by Mexican authorities who have included them as another target of the low-intensity war. Over 560 international observers, development workers and humanitarian aid representatives have been expelled from Mexico for their support of indigenous people since the 1994 uprising. Military and immigration checkpoints surround the indigenous communities in an effort to keep their global sympathizers out. Government and migration agencies have repeatedly violated international observers' rights to free transit, a fair trial and the right to have a translator and lawyer present during interrogation.

Yet despite persecution from the Mexican government, and perhaps despite the interests of their own government, US citizens keep coming to the conflict zone. They come to be witness to a war that doesn't officially exist, to give voice to a people threatened with cultural extinction and to accompany a struggle that, according to the Chiapan *campesinos*, has no borders.

—San Cristóbal de las Casas, December 2000

# CHRONOLOGY OF EVENTS IN CHIAPAS SINCE 1994[7]

## 1994: THE UPRISING

**January 1**—Start of the North American Free trade Agreement (NAFTA) between the United States, Canada and Mexico. Zapatista uprising: the Zapatista Army of National Liberation (EZLN) occupies several of the main cities in Chiapas.

**January 12**—The government declares a unilateral cease-fire and announces its intention of searching for a negotiated solution with the rebels. Estimated numbers of deaths: 145 to 1,000. Large demonstration for peace in Mexico City with approximately 100,000 participants.

**February 21 - March 2**—Dialogue for peace at the San Cristóbal cathedral between the EZLN leaders (sub-commander Marcos and 20 other commanders), Commisioner for Peace, Manuel Camacho Solis and the mediator, Samuel Ruíz, Bishop of San Cristóbal.

**March 23**—Assassination of Luís Donaldo Colosio, PRI candidate for the presidency.

**June 12**—After a process of consultation among its bases, the EZLN rejects the government proposals that came out of the dialogue at the cathedral. Manuel Camacho resigns his official position.

**August 6-9**—6,000 representatives of popular organizations from all over Mexico meet to found the National Democratic Convention in Guadalupe Tepeyac, headquarters of the EZLN.

---

[7]Information from Enlace Civil and International Service for Peace (SIPAZ).

**August 21**—PRI candidate, Ernesto Zedillo Ponce de León, is elected President of Mexico.

**September 28**—Assassination of Jose Francisco Ruíz Massieu, Secretary General of the PRI, in Mexico City.

**December 1**—Ernesto Zedillo is sworn in as President.

**December 19**—The Zapatistas break the military encirclement and establish positions peacefully in 34 autonomous municipalities containing 1,111 autonomous communities.

**December 19-20**—Financial crisis: devaluation of the peso (40%), followed by economic recession highlighted by the disappearance of thousands of enterprises and one million jobs and an important fall in the standard of living of the majority of the population. The IMF, the United States and several other countries decide to rescue Mexico in 1995, with 50 billion dollars in loans, guaranteed in part with oil reserves.

**December 24**—The EZLN and the federal government accept the mediation of the CONAI, the National Mediation Commission, presided over by Bishop Samuel Ruíz.

## *1995: VIOLENCE, BETRAYAL AND HOPE*

**January**—A meeting is held between the EZLN, CONAI and the Mexican government to discuss how to protect the EZLN during upcoming peace talks and how to guarantee dialogue with dignity.

**February 9**— "Day of Betrayal." The Mexican Army violates their cease-fire and launches an invasion into the jungle, occupying many communities, not all of which are Zapatista. More than 200,000 peasants flee their homes for fear of the Army. Many do not return until May.

**February**—Arrest warrants are issued against EZLN leaders. Many suspected collaborators are detained. Army commits many human rights violations, poisoning rivers, burning houses, killing people's animals, stealing their possessions. Some rapes of indigenous women are reported. Since this invasion happened during the time of preparing fields and planting, many communities were unable to plant. Guadalupe Tepeyac, the Zapatista *Aguascalientes*, is destroyed. Strong presence and military control established in the conflict area. In Mexico City, 100,000 people protest the Army's offensive.

**March 11**—The Law for Dialogue and Negotiation is approved and arrest warrants against EZLN leadership are suspended. This law paves the way for new talks. In an effort to cut down on human rights violations, CONAI establishes civil "peace camps" in communities that had been occupied by the army. The Commission for Concordance and Pacification (COCOPA) is established in order to help government translate signed accords into legislation. Members of various political parties serve on COCOPA with three year rotating terms. The EZLN, CONAI, COCOPA and the government hold preliminary talks to determine how, when and where to hold negotiations.

**April**—Resumption of negotiations between the Zapatistas and the governmental delegation. The negotiations stretch on for months with multiple interruptions, in San Andrés Larrainzar, also known as San Andrés Sacamch'en de los Pobres.

**August 27 - September 3**—The EZLN starts a national and international consultation to define the destiny of its struggle. More than one million people respond.

**September**—New round of negotiations in four work tables: Table 1: Indigenous Rights and Culture, Table 2: Democracy and Justice, Table 3: Welfare and Development and Table 4: Women's Rights.

**December**—Four more *Aguascalientes* are inaugurated. This provokes an increase in militarization.

## 1996: THE SAN ANDRES ACCORDS

**January 1**—The National Indigenous Forum organized by the EZLN takes place and gives birth to the National Indigenous Congress. More than 300 people from 35 indigenous groups attend.

**February 16**—The San Andrés accords on Indigenous Rights and Culture are signed by the EZLN and the Mexican government.

**March**—The Mexican government does not show up to the next set of negotiations which were to have been on Democracy and Justice, nor does it send proposals.

**May**—The EZLN suspends their participation in negotiations after consulting with its base. They focus on consolidating autonomous communities instead.

**June**—More forums are held including the Special Forum for the Reform of the State.

**July 27 - August 3**—First Intercontinental Encounter for Humanity and Against Neoliberalism, also known as the "Intergalactic Encounter" organized by the EZLN in Chiapas.

**August**—The EZLN gives 5 conditions for reestablishing talks:
1) All EZLN political prisoners must be freed.
2) The government delegation must show political will to negotiate.
3) A Security and Verification Commission should be established.
4) The San Andrés accords must be complied with.
5) The government must bring concrete proposals to the negotiating table on the topic of Democracy and Justice and commit to achieving agreements.

6) There must be an end to harassment by police and military, and all paramilitary groups must be dismantled or made public and institutionalized, made to wear uniforms, etc.

**November**—COCOPA tries to reactivate the negotiations by proposing Constitutional reforms based on the San Andrés accords.

**December**—The EZLN accepts COCOPA's proposal. The government rejects it and puts forth a proposal which is totally different from the accords signed in San Andrés.

**During 1995 and 1996**—The paramilitary group known as Paz y Justicia implements a campaign of terror in northern Chiapas. Campaign is characterized by killings, displacements, ambushes, road blockades, burning of houses, etc.

## 1997: STANDSTILL OF PEACE PROCESS

**January 11**—The EZLN rejects the Mexican government's counterproposal. The low-intensity war against Zapatista supporters and opposition groups escalates. Paramilitary groups are created in northern Chiapas and in the highlands.

**March 14**—An intercommunity dispute in San Pedro Nixtalucum (municipality of El Bosque) is put down by state police who shoot Zapatista sympathizers from pickup trucks and helicopters. Four die, many are wounded, 27 people are detained and 300 are displaced.

**April**—COCOPA and Episcopal Council of Mexico visit northern Chiapas and the First Ecumenical Meeting for Reconciliation and Peace in Chiapas is held with representatives of evangelical churches and the Catholic Church.

**April 25**—200 displaced Chol Indians from northern Chiapas break the encirclement of *Paz y Justicia* paramilitary groups with a "freedom caravan." They march to the state capital, Tuxtla Gutierrez and camp in front of the government palace for 87 days without being met by government officials.

**July 6**—In national elections, the PRI lost its absolute majority in the Chamber of Deputies. The opposition parties form an opposition block. In Mexico City, PRD candidate Cuahtemoc Cárdenas becomes Mayor. In Chiapas there are many irregularities, violence and absenteeism.

**August**—CONAI puts out a document on paramilitary activity in the state of Chiapas, denouncing the training and support of paramilitary groups in military encampments.

**September**—President Zedillo does not mention Chiapas in his State of the Union address. A second Ecumenical Meeting for Reconciliation and Peace is held in San Cristóbal. The Zapatista National Liberation Front (FZLN) is formed as the political arm of the EZLN and Zapatista delegates march to Mexico City.

**October-December**—Enlace Civil receives 10-15 denunciations every month of human rights violations or incursions made by paramilitary groups. Zapatista civilians and members of Las Abejas flee their communities in Chenalho' due to threats and intimidation. Governing authorities do nothing to investigate the reports or detain those responsible for the crimes.

**December 22**—The Acteal Massacre occurs. Forty-five children, women and men are killed and 26 more are wounded over the course of more than seven hours. The bullets are from weapons that only the Mexican Army is allowed to have. Public Security and military personnel stationed nearby do nothing to stop the massacre. Members of the government are implicated at local, state and federal levels.

## *1998: ATTACKS ON AUTONOMOUS MUNICIPALITIES/ DEPORTATION OF FOREIGNERS*

**January**—Attorney General Jorge Madrazo Cuellar states there are 12 different paramilitary groups in the state of Chiapas and that these groups promote violence in indigenous communities.

**February**—Campaign against the presence of foreigners in Chiapas intensifies. Some foreigners are expelled. Eleven political prisoners are released but 54 others remain in prison.

**April 11**—Autonomous community Ricardo Flores Magón is dismantled in a police-military operation. Political prisoners are taken and many people become refugees. Nine Mexicans detained and 12 foreigners deported. Paramilitary harassment occurs in Los Plátanos, causing the displacement of 138 people.

**April 15**—President Zedillo says that the EZLN is the primary paramilitary group in Chiapas. The Governor of Chiapas says he won't allow anymore autonomous municipalities.

**April 26**—Paramilitary group, *Paz y Justicia,* forces some 1500 Chol indigenous to abandon their lands in northern Chiapas.

**May 1**—Mexican Army dismantles autonomous municipality of Tierra y Libertad with an overwhelming show of force. Fifty-three people detained. Autonomous municipality offices destroyed.

**May 6**—A group of 120 Italian observers go to the community of Taniperlas to gather statements without being authorized by Immigration. Forty are expelled and 80 are banned from returning to Mexico in the next 10 years.

**May 28**—Mexican government releases the regulations that foreign organizations will have to comply with to do international human rights observation. Groups should have approved UN status, take no more than ten people and stay in the country for no more than ten days. They should solicit their human rights observer visa 30 days in advance.

**June 7**—Bishop Samuel Ruíz resigns as mediator and CONAI disbands because it is unable to fulfill its mission.

**June 10**—Eight civilians and two police officers die in a police-military operation to dismantle the San Juan de la Libertad autonomous municipality in El Bosque. The bodies of 3 civilians are eventually returned to the families, but they are completely mutilated.

**August 3**—The Fray Bartolomé Human Rights Center releases a report saying that there have been 57 summary executions, six political assassinations and the expulsion of more than 185 foreigners in the last six months in Chiapas.

**November**—The EZLN convokes a meeting of civil society in San Cristóbal de las Casas. Three thousand citizens attend. The EZLN reiterates its five conditions for renewing dialogue with the government.

**December**—A new police force called the Federal Preventive Police is formed. They are a completely militarized police force, trained by Spain, Chile, the United States and France. Five hundred are deployed in Chiapas.

**December 22**—More than 7,000 people attend the first anniversary commemorations of the Acteal massacre.

## 1999: OPERATIONS CONTINUE AGAINST AUTONOMOUS MUNICIPALITIES

**January 14**—Human Rights Watch denounces the continuation of torture, forced disappearances and extrajudicial executions as common practices in Mexico.

**March12 - 14**—Five thousand Zapatista delegates travel to 32 different Mexican states to promote the national Zapatista referendum planned for March 21.

**March 21**—More than 2.8 million Mexican citizens participated in the national Zapatista referendum on "Recognition of Indigenous Rights and the Ending of the War of Extermination," organized by the Zapatistas and Mexican civil society.

**April**—San Andrés Sacamch'en is invaded by 2,000 members of the Public Security Forces. Later, 3,000 unarmed people from the Zapatista support groups march in and take it back. One hundred and fifty Public Security Police are forced to leave.

**June 17**—Amnesty International invites the United States Government to investigate Julio César Ruíz Ferro, who was governor of Chiapas during the Acteal massacre and who is currently employed by the Mexican embassy in Washington, DC. Amnesty International also reports receiving continued denunciations of human rights violations committed by the Mexican Federal Army and paramilitary groups linked to the Mexican government.

**July**—Six thousand soldiers are sent to reforest the Montes Azules Bioreserve in the Lacandon rainforest. Zapatista sympathizers and other groups protest the increased militarization.

**August**—Five hundred and fifty soldiers arrive by land and parachute into the community of Amador Hernández to confront community people who are blockading the construction of a road into the rainforest. Chiapas Governor Albores Guillén and Mayor of San Cristóbal, Mariano Díaz Ochoa unleash a campaign against the presence of Mexican students and foreigners in Chiapas.

**September**—The Mexican Government, without having complied with the previously signed San Andrés Accords, announces a new proposal for dialogue in Chiapas. It is rejected by the EZLN.

A total of 55 indigenous people are found guilty of crimes related to the Acteal massacre and sentenced to 35 years in prison. Ninety arrest warrants are still pending. Eleven of them are for former state government officials and state police officers.

**September 21**—Representative of the European Community in Mexico states that the human rights situation is not important enough to block upcoming commercial accords with Mexico.

**November 24-27**—UN High Commissioner on Human Rights, Mary Robinson, makes a statement of concern about impunity, increasing militarization and poor administration of justice in Chiapas.

**November 24**—A free trade agreement is signed between Mexico and the European Union.

**December 6**—Two former public officials are sentenced to six years in the case of the Acteal massacre.

### *2000: YEAR OF GREAT CHANGES OR MORE OF THE SAME?*[8]

**January 14**—Sentences are revoked for 24 of the 55 indigenous people that are serving terms for the Acteal massacre. The judge orders that the investigation be redone.

**July 2**—Vicente Fox of the PAN party is elected President of Mexico. He is the first non-PRI president in over 70 years.

**August**—Pablo Salazar, candidate of opposition coalition, is elected governor of Chiapas. He is the first non-PRI governor in over 70 years.

---

[8]For updates, see www.sipaz.org

## *A LIST OF ORGANIZATIONS AND RESOURCES ON CHIAPAS*

### *MEXICAN ORGANIZATIONS WORKING IN CHIAPAS*

**1. Alianza Cívica:** A civil rights organization that monitors the work of local and state government officials and educates citizens. Work includes observation and dissemination of information before, during and after elections.

*Contact Information:* Diego Dugelay 31, Barrio El Cerrillo, San Cristóbal de las Casas, Chiapas, Mexico, tel: 529-678-1738, e-mail: alianchis@laneta.apc.org

**2. Chiapas Photography Project & Indigenous Photography Archives:** Education project mentioned in Chapter Two.

*Contact Information:* CIESAS Sureste, Carretera a Chamula Km 3.5, Barrio La Quinta San Martín, CP 29247, San Cristóbal de las Casas, Chiapas, Tel/fax: 529-678-5670, e-mail: sureste@juarez.ciesas.edu.mx

**3. CIAM - Centro de Investigación y Acción para la Mujer:** A women's organization working on women's rights, human rights, production projects, education and health.

*Contact Information*: Sostenes Esponda #2, Barrio Santa Lucia, San Cristóbal de las Casas, Chiapas, tel: 967-678-8352, e-mail: ciam@laneta.apc.org

**4. CIEPAC - Centro de Investigaciones Económicas y Políticas de Acción Comunitaria:** A political and economic research organization that provides information and analysis on the situation in Chiapas through electronic newsletters. It publishes books on Chiapas and gives workshops in local communities.

*Contact Information:* Eje Vial Uno No. 11, Colonia Jardines de Vista Hermosa, 29297 San Cristóbal de Las Casas, Chiapas, México, Tel/Fax: 529-678-5832, e-mail: ciepac@laneta.apc.org; web: www.ciepac.org

**5. COLEM - Colectivo de Mujeres**: A women's organization working in women's rights, legal aid to women, psychological counseling, health projects and women' health rights.
*Contact Information*: Rivera #5, Barrio Tlaxcala, San Cristóbal de las Casas, Chiapas, tel/fax: 529-678-4304, e-mail: colem@laneta.apc.org

**6. ENLACE CIVIL, A. C.**: A bridge between civil society and the autonomous communities in development, production, education and health projects, as well as in providing information from the communities to the general public.
*Contact Information:* 20 de Noviembre 36, Barrio de Mexicanos, C.P. 29240, San Cristóbal de las Casas, Chiapas, tel: 529-678-2104, tel/fax: 529-678-8465, web: www.laneta.apc.org

**7. Centro de Derechos Humanos Fray Bartolomé de las Casas:** A human rights organization that provides legal aid, education, information and human rights observation.
*Contact Information:* Calle Cuauhtémoc #12, Centro, San Cristóbal de las Casas, CP 29200, Chiapas, Mexico, tel: 529-678-3548, e-mail: cdh-bcasas@laneta.apc.org

**8. FOMMA - Fortaleza de la Mujer Maya:** An indigenous women theater group and popular theater organization. Has education and training projects for children and women. See Chapter Two.
*Contact Information:* Argentina 14, Barrio de Mexicanos, San Cristóbal de las Casas, Chiapas, tel: 529-678-6730

**9. OMIECH - Organización de Médicos Indígenas del Estado de Chiapas:** Organization of indigenous doctors working in alternative medicine with the use of medicinal plants and traditional Mayan healing techniques. It provides information, education, training, health services and marketing of medicinal products.

*Contact Information:* Calzada Salomón González Blanco #10, Colonia Morelos, San Cristóbal de las Casas, Chiapas, Mexico, Tel: 529-678-5438, e-mail: omiechlaneta@laneta.apc.org

**10. Proyecto de Medios de Comunicación en Chiapas/ Chiapas Media Project:** Working bi-nationally, provides equipment and training in media communications to create videos produced by the indigenous communities.

*Contact Information:* In US: 4834 N Springfield, Chicago, IL 60625, tel: 773-583-7728, e-mail: cmp@vida.com. In Chiapas: tel: 529-678-1684

## INTERNATIONAL ORGANIZATIONS WORKING ON/IN CHIAPAS

1. **Christian Peacemaker Teams**: An initiative of the Church of the Brethren, Mennonite and Quaker churches to support violence reduction efforts around the world. CPT has maintained a presence in Chiapas, Mexico, since June 1998.
**In US**: PO Box 6508, Chicago, IL 60680, tel: 312-455-1199, fax: 312-666-2677, e-mail: CPTMX@LANETA.APC.ORG; web page: http://www.prairienet.org/cpt/

2. **Cloudforest Initiatives**: Provides information about Chiapas, educational travel programs, community work in women's basic education and health, training/technical assistance, and fair trade coffee & artisan ironwork products. Teresa Ortiz, the author of this book, is the executive director.
**In US**: PO Box 40207, St. Paul, MN, 55104, tel: 651-592-4143, e-mail: cloudforest@hwpics.com; web: www.cloudforest-mexico.org
**In Mexico**: tel: 529-678-9049, e-mail: vamayab@laneta.apc.org

3. **Ecumenical Program on Central America and the Caribbean (EPICA)**: Publishes resources on Chiapas and leads delegations to the region.
1470 Irving St. NW, Washington DC 20010, tel: 202-332-0292, fax: 202-332-1184, e-mail: epica@igc.org; web: www.epica.org

4. **Global Exchange**: Organizes "reality tours" to Chiapas and provides information and education on the region.
**In US**: 2017 Mission Street, San Francisco, CA 94110, tel/fax: 415-255-7498, web: www.globalexchange.org
**In Mexico**: 5 de Mayo #21, Tel: 529-678-0697

5. **Mexico Solidarity Network**: A coalition of over 80 organizations struggling for human rights, economic justice and democracy in the United States and Mexico.

**In US:** 4834 N. Springfield, Chicago, IL 60625, tel: 773-583-7728, e-mail: msn@mexicosolidarity.org; web: www.mexicosolidarity.org

**6. Michigan Peace Teams:** A violence reduction organization with a permanent presence team in the northern zone of Chiapas.

**In US:** e-mail: michpeacteam@peacenet.org

**7. Resource Center of the Americas:** An organization that provides information on all of Latin America, including what goes on in Chiapas.

**In US:** 3019 Minnehaha Ave., Minneapolis, MN 55406, tel: 612-276-0788, web: www.americas.org

**8. SIPAZ - International Service for Peace:** A coalition of international organizations that provides information to the international community. A team in Chiapas accompanies Mexican groups and organizations as they work towards peace and dialogue.

**In US:** PO Box 2415, Santa Cruz, CA 95063, tel/fax: 831-425-1257, e-mail: admin@sipaz.org; web: www.sipaz.org

**In Mexico:** Calle Dr. Felipe Florez # 38, San Cristóbal de las Casas, CP 29250, Chiapas, Mexico, tel/fax: 529-678-0381

**9. Witness For Peace:** Focused on changing United States policy towards Mexico. Maintains an international team of volunteers who keep apprised of the situation in Chiapas, do independent research and host delegations.

**In US:** 1229 15th St. NW, Washington, DC 20005, tel: 202-588-1471, fax: 202-588-1472, e-mail: Witness@w4peace.org

**In Mexico:** witness@laneta.apc.org

# NEWS AND ANALYSIS BULLETINS ON CHIAPAS

**1. Chiapas 95** e-mail: chiapas@eco.utexas.edu

**2. Mexico Solidarity Network** e-mail: msn@mexicosolidarity.org; web: www.mexicosolidarity.org

**3. Prensa Nuevo Amanecer** e-mail: amanecer@aa.net

**4. SIPAZ Bulletin** e-mail: chiapas@sipaz.org; web: www.sipaz.org

**5. Schools for Chiapas** 1717 Kettner Blvd., Suite 125, San Diego, CA, 92101, tel: 619-232-2841, e-mail: mexicopeace@igc.org; web: www.igc.org/mexicopeace

**6. CIEPAC - Centro de Investigaciones Económicas y Políticas de Acción Comunitaria:** Eje Vial Uno No. 11, Colonia Jardines de Vista Hermosa, 29297 San Cristóbal de Las Casas, Chiapas, México, tel/fax: 529-678-5832, e-mail: ciepac@laneta.apc.org; web: www.ciepac.org

© Rick Reinhard

## *ABOUT THE AUTHOR*

Teresa Ortiz is a Mexican educator, writer and project coordinator, and the mother of three teen-age children. A native of Mexico City, Teresa attended the National Autonomous University of Mexico (UNAM) in the late 1960s, where she participated in the student movement of 1968. After graduation, she began teaching at an alternative high school. In the1970s, she married and moved to the United States. She graduated with a BA from South Dakota State University and did graduate studies in Education at the University of Minnesota.

Teresa has been a teacher in a variety of educational programs and non-profit organizations in Minnesota. In the early 1990s, she and her family lived in Guatemala where she worked as the co-coordinator of educational travel programs for the Center for Global Education.

Teresa has been living in Chiapas since 1995. Since 1997, she has been the Executive Director of Cloudforest Initiatives, a US non-profit organization with projects in Chiapas in the areas of information, educational travel programs, community development, education, and fair trade.

A bilingual writer, Teresa has written on the social, cultural and political situation of Chiapas and Central America for both US and Mexican periodicals. This is Teresa's first book.

## BOOKS ON WOMEN IN THE AMERICAS

**Voices and Images: Mayan Ixil Women of Chajul**
by The Association of Mayan Ixil Women with Brinton Lykes (ADMI, 2000)
Trilingual, 111 pages, $35.00

**Like the Dew that Waters the Grass: Words from Haitian Women**
by Marie M.B. Racine with Kathy Ogle (EPICA, 1999) 207 pages, $14.95

**Life out of Death: The Feminine Spirit in El Salvador**
Women in Conversation with Marigold Best and Pamela Hussey (EPICA, 1997) 192 pages, $12.95

**Guatemalan Women Speak**
by Margaret Hooks (EPICA, 1993) 133 pages, $10.95

## BOOKS ON CHIAPAS

**Unmasking the Powers:**
**The Zapatista Alternative to the Neoliberal Economics**
by Philip Wheaton (EPICA, 1998) 48 pages, $5.00

**The People's Church:**
**Bishop Samuel Ruiz of Mexico and Why He Matters**
by Gary MacEoin (Crossroads, 1996, 2000) 184 pages, $17.95

## OTHER BOOKS AVAILABLE FROM EPICA

**Red Thread:**
**A Spiritual Journal of Accompaniment, Trauma and Healing**
by Jennifer Atlee-Loudon (EPICA, 2001) 150 pages, $13.95

**Oscar Romero: Memories in Mosaic**
by María López Vigil (EPICA, 2000) 424 pages, $19.95

**Cuba: Neither Heaven Nor Hell**
by María López Vigil (EPICA, 1999) 296 pages, $15.95

### Order today!
*Write, call or e-mail us for a free catalog:*
EPICA ◆ 1470 Irving Street, NW ◆ Washington, DC 20010
epicabooks@igc.org ◆ 202/332-0292